The Complete Boating Guide to the Connecticut River

Edited by

Mark C. Borton

*The Connecticut River
Watershed Council*

Embassy Imprint, Inc.

The Complete Boating Guide to the Connecticut River

Copyright © 1986,
The Connecticut River Watershed Council, Inc.
and
Embassy Imprint, Inc.
Edited by Mark C. Borton
Book Design by Susan Smith
Cover Illustration and Maps by Robert Sorensen

Library of Congress Card Catalog No. 86–070240
ISBN 0–9616371–0–2
Printed in The United States of America
First Printing, May 1986

Connecticut River Watershed Council, Inc.

Headquarters
125 Combs Road
Easthampton, MA 01027
(413) 584-0057

Upper Valley Office
45 Lyme Road
Hanover, NH 03755
(603) 643-5672

Lower Valley Office
103 Constitution Plaza
Hartford, CT 06103
(203) 277-6914

Embassy Imprint, Inc.
Bridge Road
Haddam, CT 06438
(203) 345-2574

The Connecticut River Watershed Council wishes to acknowledge with gratitude the very generous contributions of the following institutions. Without their donations *The Complete Boating Guide to the Connecticut River* would not have been possible.

AKC Fund

Aetna Life and Casualty

Champion International Paper Company

Strathmore Paper Company

The State of Connecticut, Department of Environmental Protection

The Commonwealth of Massachusetts, Department of Commerce and Economic Development

The State of Vermont, Agency of Development and Community Affairs

The State of New Hampshire

Acknowledgments

The Connecticut River Watershed Council would like to thank the following individuals, organizations, and corporations for their assistance and expertise in producing *The Complete Boating Guide to the Connecticut River*.

Researchers, Reviewers, and Contributors:

Beckett Academy, Bruce Armentrout, Rigor Asmundson, James Barrett, R. Barringer, Deborah Borton, Terry Borton, Clark Bowlen, Philip Brown, Douglas Burt, Ned Childs, Dave Conant, Stuart Copans, Frank Crohn, Jean Curtis, Ray Danforth, Max Foldeak, Dean Fuller, Greg Isles, Carol Jessop, Ron Kaczor, Don Kuntz, Maurice La Fountain, Pam Macuen, Bob McDonald, Ross McIntyre, Dr. Robert O'Malley, Sue Ellen Panitch, Patricia Pierce, Stephen Potz, Thomas Rice, Germaine Schumacher, Lester Smith, John Stanton, Anthony Tall, Shelly Whirley, Al Wilson,

James Adamski—*Massachusetts Div. of Fisheries and Wildlife*
American Red Cross
American Whitewater Affiliation
Terry Blunt—*Massachusetts Dept. of Environmental Management*
Peter Brezosky—*New Hampshire Dept. of Fish and Game*
David Burgess—*New England Power Company*
James T. Clinton—*United States Power Squadrons
    and U.S. Coast Guard Auxiliary*
Timothy Fowler—*Hampden Paper Company*
Steven Gephard—*Connecticut Dept. of Environmental Protection*
Stephen Henry—*Massachusetts Div. Fisheries and Wildlife*
John Hickey—*Holyoke Water Power Company: Northeast Utilities*
Edward Kaynor—*UMass: Water Resources Research Center*
Boyd Kynard—*UMass: Dept. of Fisheries and Wildlife*
Roger Lamson—*White Current Corporation*
Kevin McBride—*UConn: Dept. of Anthropology*
Brenda Milkofsky—*Connecticut River Foundation*
W. Kent Olson—*The Nature Conservancy, Connecticut Chapter;
    and The American Rivers Conservation Council*
Ron Pfeffer—*Northeast Utilities*
Sidney Quarrier—*Connecticut Dept. of Environmental Protection*
Earle Roberts—*Connecticut Canoe Racing Association*
Schuyler Thomson—*American Canoe Association*
United States Coast Guard
Vermont Dept. of Forests, Parks, and Recreation

CRWC Trustees:

Jim Barnes, Sharon Francis, Astrid Hanzalek, Seth Kellogg, Sue Lantz, George Moulton, Mike Newbold, Mike Smith, Jack Soper, Ann Southworth, Bud Twining, George Watkins.

CRWC Staff:

Steve Curry, Geoff Dates, Dan Frese, Michele Frome, Betsy Katz, Joyce Kennedy, Dorothy Koziol, Carol Larocque, Bob Linck, Denise Schlener, Edward Spencer

Special thanks to Edmund T. Delaney.

Contents

Preface

Rising in the mountains near the Canadian border, the Connecticut River passes through ponds where moose graze on lily pads, down cataracts, between steep rock walls, around fields, over salt marshes, and finally through Long Island Sound and into the Atlantic Ocean. At 410 miles long, draining 11,260 square miles of land, it is the longest and largest river in New England.

The Connecticut was one of the first rivers of the New World to be explored by Europeans. Its fertile valley nourished some of the most distinguished institutions of learning in the world. The mills along the River and its tributaries fired the Industrial Revolution. But in spite of its beauty and history, the Connecticut River came to be known as the nation's most beautifully landscaped sewer.

That is changing. Thanks to the Federal Clean Air and Water acts and the efforts of thousands of individuals and of organizations like the Connecticut River Watershed Council (CRWC), most of the River is now clean enough to swim in.

The Connecticut River is an extraordinary resource. It provides water for drinking, irrigation, and industry. It generates power and is a natural route for transportation. It provides us with food and has the potential for providing much more. And the River offers almost unlimited recreational opportunities.

The Connecticut River Watershed Council is dedicated to the preservation, conservation, and management of the River as the most important natural resource in the region. We believe that the quality of life in New England is directly related to the quality of our environment, and, in particular, to the quality of the Connecticut River.

The CRWC has produced this *Guide* in hopes that more people will be able to enjoy the River and become involved in the efforts to preserve it.

The Connecticut River Watershed Council, Inc.

The Connecticut River Watershed Council (CRWC) is a nonprofit, membership-supported organization dedicated to the protection and wise use of the Connecticut River and its tributaries. The CRWC works with individuals, other organizations, corporations, and government agencies at all levels to resolve environmental problems and to plan for the future of the valley.

When the CRWC was established in 1952, the Connecticut River and many of its tributaries suffered from severe pollution. Through the efforts of many dedicated people, the River is experiencing a dramatic recovery.

The CRWC is working to clean up those parts of the River that are still polluted. Some towns in the watershed still lack adequate municipal sewage treatment plants. Many towns and cities have antiquated combined storm-water and sanitary sewers that discharge untreated wastes into the River whenever it rains. Through public education, advocacy, research, and planning the CRWC is seeking to continue the progress of cleaning up the River.

The CRWC's land conservation efforts have protected several large areas in the watershed and many key resource lands, including several islands, wetlands, and valuable wildlife areas. Areas that are important for the return of the Atlantic salmon have been sites of the CRWC's protection efforts.

Public education, an important CRWC activity, can be both fun and informative. Each year the CRWC organizes a series of canoe trips on the River. Themes include history of the valley and bird life along the River. Other trips feature fishing, camping, and picnicing.

The CRWC is organized into four state councils representing the four states of the watershed. These councils are supported by professionally staffed offices in Hanover, NH; Easthampton, MA; and Hartford, CT. We invite you to join the CRWC and help make the Connecticut River Valley a better place to live and to visit.

How To Use This Guide

Each of the 30 River-segment descriptions in this book includes four different types of information about the River and surrounding countryside: maps, summary tables, narrative descriptions, and sidebars.

Maps

Each segment begins with a map of the area of the River that is covered in the narrative description. The key to the symbols used in these maps is below. *Please note that the map scale varies.*

River or Stream

State Road ──(47)──

Federal Highway ──⟨1⟩──

Interstate Highway ──(91)──

Railroad +++++++++++++++++

Dam ◁▭▷

Town ●

Place of Interest ▮

Mountain ◮

State Boundary ── ── ── ──

Topographic Map Boundary ── ── ── ──

Trail ·······················

Location of Map in State (MA) Outline

Scale ▭▬▭

Magnetic North ⬆ N

The maps included in this book are not designed to replace the National Oceanographic and Atmospheric Administration navigational charts that should be carried on board all boats operating from Hartford south or on Long Island Sound.

Summary Tables

The second part of every segment is The Summary Table.

EXAMPLE:

a. # East Haddam to Essex

b.	MILE:	15.5-6.0 (9.5 miles).
c.	NAVIGABLE BY:	All craft with drafts less than 15' and mast heights less than 81'.
d.	DIFFICULTY:	Flat water. (Beware of tides, winds, and boat wakes.)
e.	PORTAGES:	None.
f.	CAMPING:	Mile 12.5; Gillette Castle State Park; Hadlyme, CT; (203) 526-2336.
		Mile 11.5; Selden Neck State Park; Hadlyme, CT; (203) 526-2336.
g.	USGS:	Deep River 7.5, Hamburg 7.5, Essex 7.5, Old Lyme 7.5.
h.	NOAA:	Connecticut River: Deep River to Bodkin Rock (#12377), Long Island Sound to Deep River (#12375)

KEY:

a. The section of the River that is being discussed.

b. Mileage reference points measured upriver from the Old Saybrook (CT) Lighthouse; segment length.

c. The type of boats suitable for this section of the River; i.e., kayak, canoe, powerboat, sailboat.

d. The type of water conditions that can be expected; i.e.,

Flat water:	smooth-surfaced water with slight current.
Quick water:	faster running water with some riffles and small waves.

Class I-VI: Refers to the *International Scale of River Difficulty* prepared by The American Whitewater Affiliation.

■ *Class I*—Moving water with a few riffles and small waves. Few or no obstructions.

■ *Class II*—Easy rapids with waves up to 3 feet and wide, clear channels that are obvious without scouting. Some maneuvering is required.

■ *Class III*—Rapids with high irregular waves often capable of swamping an open canoe. Narrow passages that often require complex maneuvering. May require scouting from shore.

■ *Class IV*—Long, difficult rapids with constricted passages that often require precise maneuvering in very turbulent waters. Scouting from shore is often necessary, and conditions make rescue difficult. Generally not possible for open canoes. Boaters in covered canoes and kayaks should be able to Eskimo roll.

■ *Class V*—Extremely difficult, long, and very violent rapids with highly congested routes that nearly always must be scouted from shore. Rescue conditions are difficult and there is significant hazard to life in the event of a mishap. Ability to Eskimo roll is essential for kayaks and canoes.

■ *Class VI*—Difficulties of Class V carried to the extreme of navigability. Nearly impossible and very dangerous. For teams of experts only, after close study and with all precautions taken.

e.   Location (by mile reference number) of impassable obstacle such as a dam, falls, low bridge, etc.; side of River on which to portage; length of portage.

f.   Location (by mile reference number) of established campsites; name of site; telephone number.

g.   United States Geological Survey (USGS) maps for the region. Maps come in two scales: 7.5-minute series, and 15-minute series. Maps are available from local book shops, sporting goods stores, and from the

> U.S. Geological Survey
> Eastern Region Distribution Branch
> 1200 South Eads Street
> Arlington, VA 22202
> (703) 557-2751

h. National Oceanographic and Atmospheric Administration (NOAA) navigational charts for the area. Navigational charts are available from chandleries and sporting goods stores, and the

> U.S. Commerce Department, National Ocean Survey
> Distribution Branch N/CG-33
> Riverdale, MD 20737-1199
> (301) 436-8194

Narrative Descriptions

The third part of every River segment is the narrative description of what to look for and what to look out for while on the River. The descriptions go into detail about the conditions found on the River and the area through which the River flows. These descriptions are written north to south to follow the flow of the River. For additional information about portages, access areas, and places of interest, we recommend that you read the narrative descriptions for the areas above and below the section of the River on which you will be boating.

The information in these descriptions is based on *The Connecticut River Guide* that was originally published by the CRWC in 1966. The manuscript was then updated and sent for further review to almost 100 individuals throughout the valley who have particular knowledge of and experience on various sections of the River.

Sidebars

The final part of each section is a sidebar or short article on history, geology, ecology, or whimsy that is not necessary for safe navigation but will add to your enjoyment of the River.

While we have prepared *The Complete Boating Guide to the Connecticut River* with as much care and in as much detail as possible, neither it nor any guide should be taken on blind faith. A river is in a constant state of flux. Sandbars will appear and disappear. Campgrounds and marinas will change. If during your travels on the River you note a change or some discrepancy in the text, or if you have additional information that would be useful to other boaters, please write to us so that we may include it in future editions of the *Boating Guide*. Thank you.

Boating Safety

Safety in boating, like so many other things, is a matter of common sense. However, it is our experience that "common sense" is more a developed appreciation and understanding than innate knowledge. It is for this reason that we offer these guidelines and suggestions. We hope that you will follow these suggestions until they become instinctive. No matter how experienced a boater you are, it is a good idea to review these guidelines from time to time.

Since boating on the Connecticut River can take the form of whitewater kayaking, coastal cruising, or anything in between, we have included two sets of boating-safety guidelines. For the kayaker or canoeist, we recommend familiarizing yourself with the American Whitewater Affiliation Safety Code. Sailors and powerboaters should review the U.S. Coast Guard Checklist For Safe Boating on page 18. All boaters should file a float plan (page 21) whenever they head out.

The American Whitewater Affiliation Safety Code

1 PERSONAL PREPAREDNESS AND RESPONSIBILITY

1 *Be a Competent Swimmer* with the ability to handle yourself underwater.

2 *Wear a life jacket.*

3 *Keep Your Craft Under Control.* Control must be good enough at all times to stop or reach shore before you reach any danger. Do not enter a rapid unless you are reasonably sure that you can safely navigate it or swim the entire rapid in the event of capsize.

4 *Be Aware of River Hazards and Avoid Them.* Following are the most frequent *killers.*

  A. *HIGH WATER.* The river's power and danger and the difficulty of rescue increase tremendously as the flow rate increases. It is often misleading to judge river level at the put-in. Look at a narrow, critical passage. Could a sudden rise from sun on a snow pack, rain, or a dam release occur on your trip?

  B. *COLD.* Cold quickly robs one's strength, along with one's will and ability to save oneself. Dress to protect yourself from cold water and weather extremes. When the water temperature is less than 50°, a diver's wet suit is essential for safety in the event of an upset. Next best is wool clothing under a windproof outer garment such as a splashproof nylon shell; in this case one should also carry matches and a complete change of clothes in a waterproof package. If, after prolonged exposure, a person experiences uncontrollable shaking or has difficulty talking or moving, he must be warmed immediately by whatever means available.

C. *STRAINERS*. These include brush, fallen trees, bridge pilings, or anything else that allows river current to sweep through but pins boat and boater against the obstacle. The water pressure on anything trapped in this way is overwhelming, and there may be little or no whitewater to warn of danger.

D. *WEIRS, REVERSALS, AND SOUSE HOLES*. The water drops over an obstacle, then curls back on itself in a stationary wave, as is often seen at weirs and dams. The surface water is actually going *upstream,* and this action will trap any floating object between the drop and the wave. Once trapped, a swimmer's only hope is to dive below the surface where the current is flowing downstream or to try to swim out the end of the wave.

5 *Boating Alone* is not recommended. The preferred minimum is three craft.

6 *Have a Frank Knowledge of Your Boating Ability.* Don't attempt water beyond this ability. Learn paddling skills and teamwork, if in a multiple-manned craft, to match the river you plan to boat.

7 *Be in Good Physical Condition* consistent with the difficulties that may be expected.

8 *Be Practiced in Escape* from an overturned craft, in self-rescue, in rescue, and in artificial respiration. Know first aid.

9 *The Eskimo Roll* should be mastered by kayakers and canoers planning to run large rivers and/or rivers with continuous rapids where a swimmer would have trouble reaching shore.

10 *Wear a Crash Helmet* where an upset is likely. This is essential in a kayak or covered canoe.

11 *Be Suitably Equipped.* Wear shoes that will protect your feet during a bad swim or walk for help, yet will not interfere with swimming (tennis shoes recommended). Carry a knife and wa-

terproof matches. If you need eyeglasses, tie them on and carry a spare pair. Do not wear bulky clothing that will interfere with your swimming when waterlogged.

2 BOAT AND EQUIPMENT PREPAREDNESS

1   *Test New and Unfamiliar Equipment* before relying on it for difficult runs.

2   *Be Sure Craft is in Good Repair* before starting a trip. Eliminate sharp projections that could cause injury during a swim.

3   Inflatable craft should have *Multiple Air Chambers* and should be test-inflated before starting a trip.

4   *Have Strong, Adequately Sized Paddles or Oars* for controlling the craft and carry sufficient spares for the length of the trip.

5   *Install Flotation Devices* in noninflatable craft, securely fixed, and designed to displace as much water from the craft as possible.

6   *Be Certain There is Absolutely Nothing to Cause Entanglement* when coming free from an upset craft; i.e., a spray skirt that won't release, or tangles around the legs; life-jacket buckles or clothing that might snag; canoe seats that lock on shoe heels; foot braces that fail or allow feet to jam under them; flexible decks that collapse on boaters' legs when a kayak is trapped by water pressure; baggage that dangles in an upset; loose rope in the craft, or badly secured bow/stern lines.

7   *Provide Ropes to Allow You to Hold Onto Your Craft* in case of upset, and so that it may be rescued. Following are the recommended methods:

A.   *Kayaks and Covered Canoes* should have 6-inch-diameter grab loops of ¼-inch rope attached to bow and stern. A stern painter 7 or 8 feet long is optional and may be used if properly secured to prevent entanglement.

B.   *Open Canoes* should have bow and stern lines (painters) securely attached, consisting of 8 to 10 feet of ¼- or ⅜-inch rope. These lines must be secured in such a way that they will not come loose accidentally and entangle the boaters during a swim, yet they must be ready for immediate use during an emergency. Attached balls, floats, and knots are not recommended.

C.   *Rafts and Dories* should have taut perimeter grab lines threaded through the loops usually provided.

8 *Respect Rules for Craft Capacity* and know how these capacities should be reduced for whitewater use. (Liferaft ratings must generally be halved.)

9 *Carry Appropriate Repair Materials:* tape (heating duct tape) for short trips, complete repair kit for wilderness trips.

10 *Car Top Racks Must Be Strong* and positively attached to the vehicle, and each boat must be tied to each rack. In addition, each end of each boat should be tied to the car bumper. Suction-cup racks are poor. The entire arrangement should be able to withstand all but the most violent vehicle accident.

3   LEADER'S PREPAREDNESS AND RESPONSIBILITY

1 *River Conditions.* Have a reasonable knowledge of the difficult parts of the run, or, if an exploratory trip, examine the maps to estimate the feasibility of the run. Be aware of possible rapid changes in river level, and how these changes can affect the difficulty of the run. If important, determine approximate flow rate or level. If trip involves important tidal currents, secure tide information.

2 *Participants.* Inform participants of expected river conditions and determine if the prospective boaters are qualified for the trip. All decisions should be based on group safety and comfort. Difficult decisions on the participation of marginal boaters must be based on total group strength.

3 *Equipment.* Plan so that all necessary group equipment is present on the trip: 50- to 100-foot throwing rope, first-aid kit with fresh and adequate supplies, extra paddles, repair materials, and survival equipment, if appropriate. Check equipment as necessary at the put-in, especially life jackets, boat flotation, and any items that could prevent complete escape from the boat in case of an upset.

4 *Organization.* Remind each member of individual responsibility in keeping group compact and intact between leader and sweep (capable rear boater). If group is too large, divide into smaller groups, each of appropriate boating strength, and designate group leaders and sweeps.

5 *Float Plan.* If trip is into a wilderness area, or for an extended period, your plans should be filed with appropriate authorities or left with someone who will contact them after a certain time. Establishment of checkpoints along the way at which civilization

could be contacted, if necessary, should be considered. Knowing location of possible help could speed rescue in any case.

4 IN CASE OF UPSET

1   *Evacuate Your Boat Immediately* if there is imminent danger of being trapped against logs, brush, or any other form of strainer.

2   *Recover With an Eskimo Roll if Possible.*

3   *If You Swim, Hold Onto Your Craft.* It has much flotation and is easy for rescuers to spot. Get to the upstream end so craft cannot crush you against obstacles.

4   *Release Your Craft If This Improves Your Safety.* If rescue is not imminent and water is numbing cold, or if worse rapids follow, then strike out for the nearest shore.

5   *When Swimming Rocky Rapids,* use backstroke with legs downstream and feet near the surface. If your foot wedges on the bottom, fast water will push you under and hold you there. Get to slow or very shallow water before trying to stand or walk. Look ahead. Avoid possible entrapment situations: rock wedges, fissures, strainers, brush, logs, weirs, reversals, and souse holes. Watch for eddies and slack water so that you can be ready to use these when you approach. Use every opportunity to work your way toward shore.

6   If others spill, *Go After the Boaters.* Rescue boats and equipment only if this can be done safely.

United States Coast Guard Checklist For Safe Boating

BE EDUCATED AND PREPARED:

——— *THE OVERWHELMING MAJORITY OF BOAT OPERATORS THAT HAVE FATAL ACCIDENTS HAVE NEVER TAKEN A SAFE-BOATING COURSE.* Call the toll-free number 1-800-336-BOAT for information on courses available in your locality.

——— *Carry all safety equipment required by Federal and State law.* Federal requirements are discussed in the pamphlet: "Federal Requirements for Recreational Boats," which you can get by writing to U.S. Coast Guard, Office of Boating, Public, and Consumer Affairs, Washington, DC 20593. Your State Boating Law Administrator can tell you if your state has any additional requirements. Also recommended:

___ a first aid kit
___ a pump or bailer
___ a transistor radio
___ extra fuel

___ paddle or oars
___ anchor and line
___ drinking water
___ distress flares (now a requirement in many waters)

___ *Have a Coast Guard Auxiliary Courtesy Marine Examination*—a free inspection to see if you are complying with federal and state safety requirements. The inspection is strictly confidential.

___ *Familiarize yourself and your crew with distress signals and emergency procedures.* Practice putting on personal flotation devices.

AVOID FIRES AND EXPLOSIONS:

___ 1. Handle volatile fuels carefully.
___ 2. Check with your owner's manual for proper fuel and ventilation system maintenance.
___ 3. Test and inspect for fuel leaks periodically.
___ 4. Heed regulations concerning fire extinguishers and keep them in good condition.
___ 5. *Refueling is dangerous if safety precautions are not observed:*
    a. Fill all portable tanks on dock.
    b. Moor boat securely.
    c. Extinguish cigarettes and all flames on boat and turn off all engines and electrical equipment.
    d. Close all window and door openings in galley.
    e. Keep hose nozzle grounded.
    f. Wipe up all gasoline or oil spillage.
    g. Keep fire extinguisher handy.
    h. Ventilate engine and fuel compartment and check for fumes and gas odor.
    i. Use your blower prior to getting underway.

BEFORE GETTING UNDERWAY:

___ *BE ESPECIALLY CAREFUL IF YOU HAVE A SMALL BOAT* (a boat 20′ or under). The overwhelming majority of capsizings occur on small boats because of sudden weight shifts. Any small boat can be "tippy."

___ The Coast Guard recommends that PFD's be worn by children and nonswimmers at all times. *Everyone should wear them if conditions become hazardous. THE MOST COMMON CAUSE OF*

BOATING ACCIDENT DEATHS IS DROWNING AND HY-POTHERMIA—SITUATIONS WHERE THE VICTIM MIGHT HAVE SURVIVED BY WEARING A PFD.

___ *DO NOT OPERATE BOAT IF INTOXICATED, FATIGUED OR STRESSED.* These human factors cause over 50 percent of all boating accidents. Remember that reaction time is much slower after being out in the marine environment for a few hours.

___ *KEEP A GOOD LOOKOUT.* Failure to do so causes most collisions. You need a second person to act as lookout if towing a skier.

___ *TRAVEL AT SAFE SPEEDS.* Give swimmers, skiers, and divers a wide berth.

___ *OBEY* state and federal laws, local laws and "Rules of the Road."

___ *RESPECT BAD WEATHER.* Try to get ashore if weather turns bad. NOAA weather is heard on radios with a weather band or on special weather radios on high band FM frequencies 162.40 to 162.55 MHz. Some weather radios turn on automatically if a warning is broadcast. You can get a list of weather radio manufacturers by writing to: National Weather Service (Attn: W/OM 15X2), NOAA, Silver Spring, MD 20910. You can also get the national Weather Service boating forecast phone number from Information.

IF YOU GET IN TROUBLE:

Radio for help. Use the emergency VHF channel 16 (156.8 MHz) if in trouble. (The Coast Guard also monitors CB channel 9 *whenever resources permit monitoring;* VHF channel 16 is monitored constantly.)

Everyone should wear a life preserver if conditions become hazardous.

In most capsizings, chances for survival and being found are better if you *stay with the boat* (even if you are a good swimmer). *In cold water, climb onto a capsized boat or huddle together to prevent hypothermia.*

FLOAT PLAN

Complete this page before going boating and leave it with a reliable person who can be depended upon to notify the Coast Guard or other rescue organization should you not return as scheduled. Do not file this plan with the Coast Guard.

1. Name of person reporting: _____ Phone: _____
2. Type of boat: _____ Color: _____
   Trim: _____ Registration No.: _____
   Length: _____ Name: _____ Make: _____
   Other info: _____
3. Persons aboard: Name, Address, Telephone No.:

   _____

   _____

   _____

4. Engine type: _____ H.P.: _____
   No. of engines: _____ Fuel capacity: _____
5. Survival equipment: (Check as appropriate)
   PFDs _____ Flares _____ Mirror _____ Smoke signals _____
   Flashlight _____ Food _____ Paddles _____ Water _____
   Anchor _____ Raft or dinghy _____ Other _____
6. Radio: Type: _____ Frequencies: _____
7. Trip expectations: Leaving time _____
   Starting location _____
   Finishing location _____
   Expect to return by _____
   Return no later than _____
8. Any other pertinent info: _____
9. Color, Make, Name of car: _____
   License: Car: _____ Trailer: _____
   Where parked: _____
10. If not returned by (time) _____
    CALL: _____ Phone: _____
    _____ Phone: _____
    _____ Phone: _____

Copy this form as needed.

First Aid

The following is provided as a reference only. If the situation is serious, take the victim to a hospital immediately. A list of hospitals along the Connecticut River is on page 237.

1   BREATHING DIFFICULTY

IF THERE IS NO RESPONSE, TILT THE VICTIM'S HEAD, CHIN POINTING UP. Place one hand under the victim's neck and gently lift. At the same time, push with the other hand on the victim's forehead. This will move the tongue from the back of the throat to open the airway.

IMMEDIATELY LOOK, LISTEN, AND FEEL FOR AIR. While maintaining the backward head tilt position, place your cheek and ear close to the victim's mouth and nose. Look for the chest to rise and fall while you listen and feel for the return of air. Check for about 5 seconds.

IF THE VICTIM IS NOT BREATHING, GIVE FOUR QUICK BREATHS. Maintain the backward head tilt, pinch the victim's nose with the hand that is on the victim's forehead to prevent leakage of air; open your mouth wide, take a deep breath, seal your mouth around the victim's mouth, and blow into the victim's mouth with four quick but full breaths as fast as you can. When blowing, use only enough time between breaths to lift your head slightly for better inhalation. For an infant, give gentle puffs and blow through the mouth and nose and do not tilt the head back as far as an adult. If you do not get an air exchange when you blow, reposition the head and try again.

AGAIN, LOOK, LISTEN, AND FEEL FOR AIR EXCHANGE.

IF THERE IS STILL NO BREATHING, CHANGE RATE TO ONE BREATH EVERY 5 SECONDS FOR AN ADULT.

FOR AN INFANT, GIVE ONE GENTLE PUFF EVERY 3 SECONDS.

MOUTH TO NOSE METHOD. The mouth to nose method can be used with the sequence described above instead of the mouth to mouth method. Maintain the backward head tilt position with the hand on the victim's forehead. Remove the hand from under the neck and close the victim's mouth. Blow into the victim's nose. Open the victim's mouth for the look, listen, and feel step.

FIRST AID FOR CHOKING

If victim can cough, speak, breathe ➡ Do not interfere

If victim cannot
    cough   *Have someone call for help.*
    speak
    breathe
       ⬇

TAKE ACTION: FOR CONSCIOUS VICTIM

Repeat steps until effective or until victim becomes unconscious.

TAKE ACTION: FOR UNCONSCIOUS VICTIM

←Repeat steps until effective.←

Continue artificial ventilation or CPR, as indicated.

2   BLEEDING—Bleeding may be stopped by applying firm pressure directly over the wound to form clotting or by digital pressure on a pressure point in the affected arm or leg or by a tourniquet (only if neccessary) or by a combination of these.

3   POISONING

First Aid for Conscious Victim of Poisoning

1 Dilute the poison by having the victim drink a glass of water or milk, if the victim is conscious and not having convulsions. Discontinue dilution if it makes the victim nauseous.

2 Save the label or container of the suspected poison for identification. If the victim vomits, save a sample of the vomited material for analysis.

3 Seek medical assistance by calling the poison control center or a physician. You should post poison control center number for your region on your telephone. If you do not have the number, dial O (operator) or 911.

4 If the victim becomes unconscious, keep his or her airway open. Give artificial respiration or cardiopulmonary resusitation (CPR), if indicated. Call an emergency squad as soon as possible. (Also see "First Aid for Unconscious Victim.")

First Aid for Unconscious Victim of Poisoning
1 Maintain an open airway.
2 Call for an emergency squad as soon as possible.
3 Administer artificial respiration and CPR, if indicated.
4 Save the container of the suspected poison.
5 If the patient has vomited, save a sample of the vomited material.
6 Do not give fluids to an unconscious person.
7 Do not induce vomiting in an unconscious person. If the victim is vomiting, position him or her on his or her side and turn the person's head so that the material drains out of the mouth.

4   ANIMAL BITES—Wash wound thoroughly, using a solution of soap and water. Rinse with clean running water. Apply sterile dressing. Always consult a physician at once. Confine animal to escapeproof quarters. Notify police.

5   BRUISES—Apply ice bag or cold pack. If skin is broken, treat as a minor cut.

6   BURNS AND SCALDS—For burns of limited extent: Apply cold water. Cover with sterile dressing. For extensive burns: Treat for shock. Remove loose clothing. Do not remove clothing which sticks to burned area. Consult a physician. Never apply oil, butter, or any preparation to a burn. If burn covers a considerable area or if fever or blisters develop, see a physician.

7   CUTS—Wash with soap and water. Wash away from—not into—the cut. Apply direct pressure over cut with sterile gauze until bleeding stops. Apply antibacterial ointment and sterile dressing.

8   EYES—Foreign bodies: Remove only those foreign bodies lying on the surface of the eye. Lift off with the corner of a clean handkerchief or flush eye with water, using eye dropper or bulb syringe. Do not rub eye. Never remove anything embedded in eyeball. Consult physician.

9 FAINTING—Keep person lying down with head slightly lowered. Loosen any tight clothing about neck. If person does not respond within a short time, summon physician.

10 FRACTURES—Deformity of injured part usually means fracture. If fracture is suspected, do not attempt to move injured person. Call physician at once. Treat for shock.

11 FROSTBITE AND CHILLS—Handle gently to avoid injury. Bring person into warm room and give warm drink. Immerse body part in lukewarm but not hot water or gently wrap in warm blankets. Do not rub or expose to stove or fire, nor put in hot water. Such procedures may cause serious permanent damage.

12 HEAT CRAMPS—Symptoms: cramps in muscles of abdomen and extremities. Treatment: Same as for heat exhaustion.

13 HEAT EXHAUSTION—Symptoms: Cool, clammy skin with body temperature about normal or below. Treatment: Keep person lying down with head lowered. If conscious, give salt-water solution to drink (1 teaspoon of salt to 1 glass of water) in small amounts at frequent intervals.

14 HEAT STROKE—Symptoms: Hot, dry skin and extremely high body temperature. Treatment: Repeatedly sponge bare skin with cool water or rubbing alcohol or apply cold packs or place person in a tub of cold water (do not add ice) until body temperature is sufficiently lowered. Do not give stimulants. Consult a physician immediately.

15 INSECT BITES—Remove stinger if present. Apply cold applications and soothing lotions, such as calamine. If person has history of allergic reactions to insect bites, get him to a physician at once.

16 NOSEBLEED—Place person in chair with head erect. Loosen clothing at neck. Saturate towel with ice water and apply over bridge of nose, at same time holding nostrils together tightly. Keep changing cold towels at intervals of one minute. If blood continues to flow freely, send for physician at once.

17 POISON IVY—Wash exposed area well with naphtha (yellow) soap. Do not use brush or other rough material. Then use rubbing alcohol, if available. Apply calamine lotion. If area spreads, swells, or forms large blisters, see a physician.

18 PUNCTURE WOUNDS—Encourage bleeding by mild pressure around the wound. Treat same as cuts. Always see a physician. A tetanus injection is usually neccessary.

19 SCRAPES—Wash with soap and water. Blot dry and treat the same as cuts. If scrape is deep and dirty, see a physician.

20 SHOCK—Keep person lying down. Cover only enough to prevent body heat loss. Get medical help.

21 SPLINTERS—Wash area with soap and water. Sterilize needle point by passing it through a flame and use it to tease out splinter. Apply antibacterial ointment and sterile dressing.

22 SPRAINS—Elevate injured part to minimize swelling and apply ice bags or cold cloths immediately after injury. Cold applications of Epsom salts may be repeated every two hours. If swelling is pronounced, do not attempt to use injured part until seen by a physician.

23 STRAINS—Apply heating pad or heat lamp, then warm, wet application to affected area. Bed rest is indicated. If strained back, place board under the mattress for firm support.

24 TOOTHACHE—If cavity is present, moisten small piece of cotton with oil of cloves and apply to cavity. If no cavity is present, apply ice bag or hot water bottle to cheek for comfort. For any toothache, always consult your dentist.

25 UNCONSCIOUSNESS—Never attempt to give anything by mouth. Never attempt to induce vomiting. Place patient lying on side with head on arm. Loosen tight clothing; maintain body heat with blanket. Summon a physician at once. Be sure patient is breathing. If not, give artificial respiration.

Illustrations reprinted with permission of the American Red Cross.

The River

The Geology of the Valley

The geologic history of the Connecticut River Valley reflects the history of the Earth itself. It all started about 4.6 billion years ago with the formation of the Earth—at least that is the current belief of geologists. More recently—some 400 to 250 million years ago—the Earth went through another traumatic experience when the continents of North America, South America, Africa, and Europe bumped into each other, forming the supercontinent known as Pangaea. This collision was not a sudden event. The continents moved at the blistering speed of a couple of inches each year. However, the severity of the collision was such that it created a range of mountains 5 to 7 miles high. These were the ancient Appalachian Mountains. The backbone of the Appalachian Mountains gives the Connecticut River Valley its basic shape and its north-south orientation.

About 200 million years ago the supercontinent started to split apart. Several enormous cracks formed before the continents finally pulled apart and the oceans flowed in to complete the separation. One of the largest of these cracks gave the Connecticut River Valley its second most recognizable feature, the wide central floodplain of the Pioneer Valley.

For a few million years, while the central valley was slowly being filled and leveled with sediment from the rest of the basin, New England had a tropical climate. Lush vegetation covered the countryside, and dinosaurs roamed the land, leaving their tracks in the soft brown mud at Cromwell, CT, and Hadley, MA. But about 65 million years ago the dinosaurs vanished. We still do not know why.

About 2 to 3 million years ago another geologic process began that had a profound effect on the Connecticut River Valley. Huge amounts of snow started building up in northern Quebec and Newfoundland. There was so much snow that it compacted itself into ice, and spread south. These glaciers were up to 2 miles thick and at one time covered all of eastern Canada and most of the northern United States. So much water was locked up in the ice sheets that the oceans dropped 200 feet.

As the glaciers moved south, they greatly accelerated the slow erosion of the landscape by wind and rain. The glaciers acted like a phalanx of the world's biggest bulldozers, smoothing off mountains, filling in and digging out valleys, dragging boulders hundreds of miles, and spreading debris (till) everywhere.

And then they stopped. The climate began to warm, and the glaciers melted. At the southern end of the glacier (the terminal moraine), an enormous pile of debris was left as the glacier receded. This sandpile and the bedrock beneath it is known as Long Island. As the glacier melted and haltingly crept back north, it left several other (recessional) moraines and deltas along the way. The most significant of these deltas formed in the vicinity of Cromwell, CT.

The local topography of Cromwell was such that the delta formed a natural dam across the entire drainage basin, trapped the meltwater behind it, and created a gigantic lake that extended all the way to Lyme, NH. Lake Hitchcock, as it is now called, was 170 miles long and up to 8 miles wide. For the few thousand years that Lake Hitchcock existed, the annual winter dry season and summer runoff deposited layer after layer of fine and course sediment (varved deposits), slowly leveling the bottom of the lake.

Eventually, the natural dam at Cromwell broke. Lake Hitchcock was drained, leaving what we now recognize as the Connecticut River Valley. Where the lake bed had been lay a broad and fertile plain. The plain was further leveled and enriched by periodic flooding. This process created the rich agricultural fields of the Pioneer Valley that first attracted the American colonists. Many believe that the glaciers were also responsible for the sandbar at the River's mouth. But in fact, it is the action of the prevailing winds, currents, and tides that created and maintain the sandbar at Old Saybrook that so troubled early sailors.

Where the River flowed through mountainous areas, such as in the upper valley, it was confined by the bedrock and took the fastest route to the sea. This created a fairly narrow and straight river. In areas where the terrain was more level, such as the Pioneer Valley, the current was slower and more easily diverted from its straight path. Shallow loops, or meanders, were formed. Once started, these loops had a tendency to become more and more exaggerated. Eventually the meanders doubled back on themselves, cutting short the loop and leaving an island and an "oxbow lake." There are several excellent examples of oxbows on the Connecticut River, most notably at Wethersfield, CT; Northampton, MA; and North Haverhill, NH.

In the last 300 years another force has made a profound impact on the geology of the Connecticut River Valley. In that time, man has carved roads and built dikes. We have blasted away mountains and dammed the River. But 300 years on man's calendar is but a few seconds of the geologic year. Nevertheless, the combined effects of man's constructive and destructive energies coupled with a predicted 1-foot rise in the level of the ocean in the next 30 years because of the "greenhouse effect" suggests that our geologic environment is presently changing as fast as, possibly faster than, it ever has before.

The History of the Valley

The first evidence of human occupation of the Connecticut River Valley dates from 10,000 years ago. Little is known of these so-called Paleo-Indians other than that they were big game hunters. As the climate and associated flora and fauna changed, the lives of the humans also changed. While still nomadic, these native Americans exploited the increasingly diverse plant and animal resources of the area. About 1,000 years ago, the Indians of southern New England began to cultivate corn, beans, and squash.

With the advent of horticulture came a semipermanent life-style. Groups would establish a village base along a river that served as a major food source and trade and transportation route. From here they would make trips to hunt, fish, gather raw materials for tools and utensils, and trade with other Indian groups. Local Indians were still practicing this seminomadic life-style when European settlers first began to trade in and occupy the Connecticut River Valley.

The Dutch explorer Adrian Block was the first European to explore the River, sailing to the head of navigation at the Enfield Rapids in 1614. Some years later, the Dutch established trading posts at Saybrook and Hartford. To satisfy the demand for furs, the Europeans paid the Indians to trap as many beaver, fox, and mink as could be found. In return, the Indians usually received metal or cloth products.

The first English settlers sailed from Massachusetts to Windsor in 1633. Other settlements were established in Wethersfield in 1634 and Saybrook in 1635. The next year Thomas Hooker settled Hartford and Thomas Pynchon came to Agawam, now Springfield. Only three years after his arrival, Hooker promulgated the Fundamental Orders, the first formal adoption in the American colonies of the principles of self-government based on "the free consent of the people." The English and the Dutch had conflicting claims on the valley, but in 1654 the Dutch were ousted and the English took complete control.

In the ensuing years the various settlements expanded: Saybrook soon encompassed Lyme, Essex, Westbrook, Deep River, and Chester; from Hartford and Wethersfield there was a move downriver to Cromwell, Middletown, and the Haddams; from Springfield, groups moved northward to Northampton, Hadley, Deerfield, and Greenfield. The northernmost settlements saw frequent Indian attacks that culminated in King Philip's War in 1675 and the virtual extermination of the Indians in southern New England.

The end of the 17th century brought peace and prosperity in the lower River valley. In the upper valley, however, there were numerous conflicts between the English settlers and the Indians, who were allied with the French in Canada. The most famous of these conflicts was the Deerfield Massacre of 1704.

The second quarter of the 18th century saw the expansion of the settlements in the upper valley. Settlements initially took the form of forts: Fort Dummer near Brattleboro in 1725, Bellows Falls in 1735, and four years later, Rockingham and Westminster. Charlestown, NH, was the site of the famous Fort No. 4 where a French and Indian attack was repulsed in 1747. It was also to Fort No. 4 that Robert Rogers returned with his Rangers after a punitive raid on the St. Francis Indians of Quebec.

In the 1760's the so-called New Hampshire Grants opened up much of the land on both sides of the River, leading to the settlement of Lebanon, Hanover, and Lyme on the eastern side, and Windsor, Springfield, and St. Johnsbury in the west. Vermont, as such, did not then exist. There were numerous conflicting jurisdictional claims by Massachusetts, New Hampshire, and New York in which Ethan Allen and the Green Mountain Boys played a leading role. These differences were not resolved until after the Revolutionary War, with the admission of Vermont as the 14th state of the Union. In fact, boundary disputes between Vermont and New Hampshire continued until 1933, when the Supreme Court set markers on the Vermont side of the River, creating an unusual situation in which New Hampshire owns the River, and must maintain the bridges across it. The historical precedent for this action was that in 1764 King George III of England had ruled that all lands as far as the "western banks of the River Connecticut" shall be part of New Hampshire.

The lower valley was little affected by the wars and problems of the upper valley. Prosperity and improving the quality of life were the important issues in the towns along the River in Massachusetts and Connecticut. Agriculture was the main occupation, rivaled only by shipbuilding in the River towns south of Windsor, CT. Middletown was the most important port in Connecticut and a leading shipping center for the West Indies trade. With a population of 5,564, it was the largest and wealthiest town on the River. The growth of the River trade prompted the Connecticut General Assembly to take action in 1773 to mark the channels and sandbars by authorizing a lottery to raise funds for that purpose.

There was little military action in the Connecticut River Valley during the American Revolution, but privateers from the River towns of Hartford, Middletown, East Haddam, and Essex helped by preying on British shipping. The first American-built warship, the *Oliver Cromwell,* was built in Essex. The most important contribution of the valley to the revolutionary cause was in the form of provisions and supplies. In an effort directed by Hartford's Jeremiah Wadsworth, hundreds of tons of food and ammunition were transported to Washington and his troops at Valley Forge. In 1771, Washington and Rochambeau of France met at Wethersfield to plan the campaign that culminated in the surrender of Cornwallis at Yorktown. After the Revolution, men such as General Henry Knox of Springfield, Chief Justice Oliver Ellsworth of Windsor, lexicographer Noah Webster of Hartford, the Wolcotts, and many others from the River valley continued to play influential roles in the development of the United States.

In 1786, economically displaced farmers lead by Daniel Shays of Pelham, MA, rebelled against the Massachusetts court, demanding the restructuring of the tax system. On February 2, 1787, Shays was forced to flee to safety in Vermont with the death penalty awaiting his return to Massachusetts. The call for a national constitutional convention and the establishment of a strong central government were in part a reaction to Shays' Rebellion and the states' inability to deal with such cases individually.

General prosperity followed until 1806 when President Jefferson imposed an international trade embargo that spelled financial disaster for many of the seafaring towns of the lower valley. The only encounter of the War of 1812 to take place along the River was the 1814 British raid on Essex, CT, where some 23 ships were burned.

The Connecticut River Valley can well be said to be the birthplace of the Industrial Revolution in America. By the early 19th century there were scores of small factories throughout the valley powered by the flowing water of the Connecticut River and its tributaries. However, the valley's most important contribution was the development of the concept of interchangeable parts. This technological breakthrough led to the machine-tool and small-arms industries of Middletown and Hartford in Connecticut, of Springfield in Massachusetts, and of Windsor in Vermont. Holyoke, MA, has the distinction of being the first planned industrial community in the United States. In 1849 a dam was constructed across the River to divert the water into three canals. Mills along the canals used the water to generate mechanical power or as process water.

It was during these years that the valley became home to numerous educational institutions. By 1810 Dartmouth College (chartered 1769) in Hanover, NH, had become one of the leading colleges in the country. The Hartford School for the Deaf, the oldest school for the disabled in the United States, was founded in 1817. Amherst College in Massachusetts followed in 1821, Trinity College in Hartford in 1823, and Wesleyan in Middletown in 1830. Mount Holyoke opened in 1837 as a seminary for women and became one of the outstanding colleges of the region. Smith College in Northampton, MA, was founded in 1873.

As early as 1787, John Fitch of South Windsor, CT, had successfully operated a steam-powered boat. Five years later, Samuel Morey ran a steamboat from Orford, NH, to Fairlee, VT. In 1822, regularly scheduled steamboat service between Hartford and New York was inaugurated, with stops at intervening towns. The building of the Windsor Locks Canal in 1829 permitted steamboat service between Hartford and Springfield. The railroads, however, were fierce competition for the steamboats, and most steamboat runs were abandoned after the arrival of the rails. The Hartford-to-New York run was the last to go, in 1931.

New England as a whole, and with it the Connecticut River Valley, prospered during the end of the 19th century. The greatly expanded cities were graced with fine public buildings, parks, churches, libraries, theaters, and museums. There were many prominent literary figures living in the valley: Lydia Sigourney, Mark Twain, and Harriet Beecher Stowe in Hartford; Samuel Bowles in Springfield; Emily Dickinson in Amherst; Edward Bellamy in Chicopee; Henry James in Northampton; Rudyard Kipling in Brattleboro. The artists Thomas Cole and Frederick Church came from Hartford. Augustus Saint-Gaudens, perhaps America's foremost sculptor, was part of a colony of artists in Cornish, NH. In the early 1900's, an artists colony of American Impressionists thrived in Old Lyme, CT. Many of their works are still to be seen in the Florence Griswold Museum there. William Gillette, famed as an actor and playwright, built his stone castle on a bluff overlooking the River in Hadlyme, CT. Middletown, Old Lyme, and Cornish were at one time or another home to Woodrow Wilson, and it was to Northampton that Calvin Coolidge returned at the end of his Presidency.

Unfortunately, the economic prosperity of the present century was accompanied by the gross neglect and abuse of the River. Raw sewage and industrial wastes were dumped into the River. Pollution had a severe impact on the already decimated fish populations. Riverbanks in urban areas were disfigured with rubbish dumps and broken-down factories. The floodplain development radically changed the dynamics of the River, greatly increasing the severity of the floods of 1927, 1936, and the hurricane of 1938, as well as several floods within the last decade.

In the last 30 years, however, a new awareness of the importance of the River has developed. The River is now being recognized as an economic resource, but, more important, as an amenity to life that should be valued for its beauty, environmental uniqueness, and recreational opportunites. Cities such as Springfield, Hartford, and Middletown have made considerable strides in reclaiming their riverfronts. With the success achieved so far in the cleaning and preservation of the River, we can look optimistically—if cautiously—to the future.

Water Quality and the Connecticut River Basin*

At one time the Connecticut River was called the nation's most beautifully landscaped sewer. It carried tons of industrial and municipal wastes. Fish died in it and people shunned it.

During the 1970's environmental legislation and government funds began to change that, halting the River's decline. Though the problems have not been entirely cured, the River and many of its tributaries have been nursed back to health. While the waters cannot be drunk—perhaps they will never meet that standard— they generally can be counted on for safe swimming and fishing.

This change resulted primarily from two major federal water-pollution acts of the 1970's, under which the Federal Government established a system of water-quality standards. States had to apply the system to set water-quality goals for portions of rivers and streams within their boundaries. The Federal Government then paid for up to 85 percent of the cost of the sewer systems and sewage-treatment plants needed to meet the goals. States and municipalities contributed the remainder. The goals are spelled out in a classification system: Class A water is safe to drink; Class B is safe for swimming and fishing; Class C is safe only for industrial use; and Class D water is unsafe for any of these uses. The water quality for nearly all the basin's rivers and streams is Class B.

The improvements have been dramatic. Five times as much of the Connecticut River meets water-quality standards now as did in 1969. New construction of, and improvements to, sewage-treatment plants in municipalities account for nearly all of the cleansing of the basin's rivers. Industries have also built their own treatment plants or lines to carry their wastes to municipal treatment plants.

Nevertheless, problems remain. Difficulties in raising funds to upgrade or build sewage-treatment plants has thrown several municipalities off the schedules set by federal law.

The major pollution problem affecting the Connecticut River today is combined drains for sewage and storm-water runoff that cause certain municipalities to empty raw sewage into the River after heavy rains. The problem is particularly acute from Holyoke, MA, south to Middletown, CT. In this area 10 communities—Holyoke, Chicopee, Springfield, West Springfield, and Agawam, MA; and Enfield, Hartford, West Hartford, Portland, and Middletown, CT—are major sources of pollution. Unfortunately, funding is scarce for separation of combined storm and sanitary sewers.

Operation and maintenence of sewage-treatment plants is another concern. No funding for this purpose is authorized by the federal water-quality acts, so this is a strictly local responsibility.

The various pollution sources are responsible for high levels of coliform bacteria, an indication of a potential health hazard and the main reason the River does not meet water-quality standards in certain areas. Other pollution problems include low dissolved oxygen levels and toxic chemicals from industrial discharges.

* Excerpt from *Recovering the Valley: Connecticut River Basin Environmental Status Report 1970-1983*. Rutherford H. Platt, Project Director. Connecticut River Watershed Council, Easthampton, MA, 1984.

Fisheries of the River

The Connecticut River has the most diverse fish population of all streams in New England. It includes native fish, fish that have been introduced, freshwater fish, saltwater visitors from Long Island Sound, and anadromous fish—species that hatch in fresh water, mature in salt water, and return to fresh water to spawn.

In the northern stretches of the stream the River is dominated by trout: brown, rainbow, and brook. In the middle portion of the River there is good fishing for cool-water species such as bass and walleye. In the lower reaches, anglers capitalize on largemouth bass, panfish, northern pike, catfish, eel, carp, white perch, and sometimes striped bass. Often the numerous coves and inlets along the lower River are the most productive areas for many of the game-fishing species, although bait-fishing in the main channel during the summer rarely fails to produce good and varied catches.

In colonial days the Connecticut River was fabulously abundant with salmon, shad, sturgeon, and other anadromous fish. Salmon up to 30 pounds and more were reported being taken in considerable numbers, and thousands of barrels of shad were put up for the Revolutionary army. Shad were so abundant that they were used as fertilizer, and indentured servants' contracts stipulated that they were not to be fed shad more than so many times a week. The salmon run was estimated to be about 40,000 fish per year, and the shad run may have included as many as 7 million fish every year.

The building of dams on the upper River and its tributaries in the early 1700's blocked off most of the salmon's spawning grounds. The construction of a dam across the River at Turner's Falls, MA, in 1798 eliminated the rest, causing the extermination of salmon and reducing the shad run considerably. Pollution in the form of sewage and industrial waste made the situation even more desperate.

The return of the Atlantic salmon has been slow. In 1870, the states of Maine, New Hampshire, Massachusetts, and Connecticut tried to reintroduce salmon to the River, but were unsuccessful because of technical and managerial problems. The effort was taken up again in 1967 with the passage of the Anadromous Fish Restoration Act, which provided federal aid for the project. In addition, fish ladders have been constructed by the power companies on all of the mainstream dams as far north as Bellows Falls, VT. At the time of this writing, construction has begun on a fish ladder around the Wilder Dam in Hartford, VT, 212 miles up the Connecticut River.

That was the expensive part. The hard part was getting the fish to cooperate. The problem was the salmon's keen sense of smell and innate homing ability. These traits allowed the salmon to swim through thousands of miles of ocean and then return to the Connecticut River to spawn, but also kept imported baby fish from believing that the Connecticut River was where they were supposed to be.

The restoration project began with salmon eggs from northern Canada. However, these eggs proved unsatisfactory because they were from an area too far north, and the fish had difficulty adapting to the Connecticut River, which was the southernmost river in which salmon spawned. After 11 years of trying with the eggs from Canada, only 11 fish had returned. Eggs from the Penobscot River in Maine were then tried. In the first year, 88 fish returned. Nearly 20 years and $60 million later, approximately 1,000 adult salmon are expected to return to the River in 1986 and are being captured by state biologists and bred in "protective custody." As the run increases, surplus fish will be allowed to swim upstream and spawn naturally. In June of 1985, a salmon swam up the fish ladder at Bellows Falls and became the first salmon to travel that far north in nearly 200 years. But control your appetite: These fish are protected by law. Any angler who catches one is required to release it unharmed. A salmon population large enough to support sport fishing may exist in the 1990's.

Because the shad were never totally eradicated from the River, their return has been much speedier. Thousands of sport fishermen participate in the annual Shad Derby, and there are enough shad to support a commercial fishing industry. No longer regarded as something to be tossed into the ground as fertilizer, shad and shad roe are now a real delicacy that is looked forward to with the coming of spring. Many towns along the River have annual-shad bake festivals that attract large crowds. The art of removing the 1,500 bones of the shad is a closely held secret that is passed down from one generation to the next.

Determined and persistent efforts to abate pollution and cleanup the River have also played an important part in the development of better fishing in the Connecticut River. However, several municipalities along the River are still without sewage treatment plants, and a variety of industrial wastes continue to be dumped into the River.

Fishing licenses are required for all areas of the River except south of the railroad bridge at Old Saybrook, CT, and are valid only in the state in which they were issued. Residents of New Hampshire and Vermont do not need a license to fish in the Connecticut River in their home states. Nonresidents need a New Hampshire license to fish in the River below the officially recognized low-water mark on the Vermont side (essentially all of the River). Since this law was established before the construction of the reservoirs, and since the low-water mark is underwater in these areas, a Vermont fishing license is technically required. Because the regulations concerning seasons, fees, and creel and tackle limits vary, we suggest that you contact the agency listed in the Appendix that has jurisdiction in the area in which you plan to fish.

Birds of the Connecticut River Valley

The Connecticut River Valley provides a diverse range of habitats for resident species of birds and considerable opportunities for migrating species to rest and feed on the way north or south. In the most northern reaches of the upper valley, spruce and fir forests provide breeding habitat for many Canadian zone species not found farther south. In the southern half of the upper valley and northern Massachusetts, the transitional Alleghenian zone predominates, with a mix of deciduous trees, white pine, and hemlock that provides habitat for a wide assortment of birds. With its broad floodplain, the lower valley provides a distinctly different habitat for waterfowl, marsh and shore birds, and grass and farmland species. As the River moves toward and into Connecticut, the southern Carolinian zone begins to take over and a new set of species is found. Below Middletown, the River leaves the fertile valley and cuts through low eastern hills for 20 miles before reaching Long Island Sound. Here the coastal species attain dominance.

The Upper Valley

The elevation of the Fourth Connecticut Lake is 2,500 feet above sea level, and although the River drops to 1,700 feet by the time it reaches First Lake, the surrounding mountains rise 3,000 to 5,000 feet. These high elevations are the home of the common loon, ring-necked duck, common goldeneye, and hooded and common merganser. In the forests are the bird-eating accipiter hawks and the little saw-whet owl. Great blue heron, American bittern, and snipe nest around the wetlands and beaver ponds. The fearless gray jay rules the campsites and picnic areas, and the raven's croak is heard on the cliff sides. The star of the coniferous forest is the warbler family: colorful little flyers, ever active in search of insects to feed to their young before they have to leave on the long flight back to the tropics.

The Central Valley

The pool above the Turner's Falls Dam is one of the best sites for waterfowl in the spring. In the summer and early fall the daily rise and fall of the water level from the pumping project makes the pool an excellent spot for wading birds.

The most bird-rich part of the valley in Massachusetts is probably the central basin from Deerfield to Northampton. There are large marshes adjoining the Deerfield River in Old Deerfield. Farther south the Bradstreet Marshes in Hatfield are formed by an old oxbow of the River. In Northampton, the Arcadia Marshes and the east and west meadows provide low floodplain habitat. All these areas attract a great variety and number of birds.

The southern lowland is divided by the central ridge into a western area drained by the Westfield and Farmington rivers and an eastern area drained by the Connecticut River. There are extensive flood pools, fields, and marshes at the Stebbin's Wildlife Refuge in Longmeadow, at Holyoke Cove in Agawam, and in South Windsor. Forest Park in Springfield is a favorite spot for migrant land birds. The exposed shoreline of the Connecticut River between Longmeadow and Agawam attracts a wide variety of birds during the summer and fall.

Arriving in the central valley as the water warms are both diving and dabbling ducks as well as great blue herons and ospreys. The marshes in Deerfield, Hatfield, Northampton, Longmeadow, and South Windsor are good for sora, Virginia rail, and American bittern. The River and adjacent ponds also attract hordes of early swallows, particularly cliff swallows, and a few purple martins.

Bradley Field, Westover, Barnes, and Turner's Falls airfields have a limited population of upland sandpiper and grasshopper sparrow. A few horned larks and vesper sparrows reside in the intensively farmed areas of the floodplain. Kingfishers and black swallows are regulars along the River and near other streams and ponds. Nighthawks buzz in the twilight over the urban centers.

Along the River from mid-July to mid-September great and snowy egrets and black-crowned night herons are regulars. Ring-billed gulls are abundant, and Bonaparte's gulls are fairly frequent. Common, black, and forester's terns have also been sighted.

Starting in September, the marshes in Deerfield, Hatfield, Northampton, Longmeadow, and South Windsor are gathering places for hundreds of dabbling ducks, many of which stay until late October or early November. Harvested or already plowed fields regularly attract golden plovers, yellowlegs, snipe, and pectoral sandpipers. Harriers begin to course the meadows, and an occasional merlin is spotted streaking across the sky. Water pipits may be found in the barrier fields, and tree and barn swallows congregate here for the last push south. Only a few diving ducks stop in this area, mosty on the River itself.

As the season progresses, the winter species begin to arrive: accipiters, rough-legged hawks, lapland longspurs, snow buntings, and, during flight years, flocks of redpolls. The herring, great black-backed, and ring-billed gulls feed at the landfills by the thousands and are joined by a few Iceland and glaucous gulls. Bald eagles visit the River during intense cold spells, especially near the rapids, where the water remains open. Mallards, black ducks, and Canada geese will stay on late-freezing ponds or on the River if there is limited snow cover and food is available nearby.

The Central Ridge

The central ridge in the lower valley ranges from 300 to 900 feet high and appears to be a trap or corridor for birds. The Mt. Tom Reservation in Holyoke and Easthampton is the largest accessible area for birding. Hawks are the most famous specialty here. The large fall flights are traditionally observed from Goat's Peak. Most migrants do not follow the ridge, but rather use the updrafts on the west side, coming in close for easy viewing. The most common migrant is the broad-winged hawk, of which hundreds or thousands can be seen in a single day. There are also a number of sharp-shinned hawks, ospreys, red-tailed hawks, and American kestrels. Migrating snow geese and double-crested cormorants are also regularly seen from the lookouts.

The best places to visit besides Mt. Tom are the various reservoirs and parks in West Hartford, Robinson State Park in Agawam, and Ashley ponds in Holyoke. The extensive spruce plantings at these locations are good sites in winter for the finch as well as the boreal chickadee, red-breasted nuthatch, golden-crowned kinglet, and pine siskin.

The Tidal River

All the water birds and southern species already discussed become common at the mouth of the River. The marshes and estuaries of Old Saybrook and Old Lyme are a stronghold for the double-crested cormorant, great blue heron, great and snowy egret, black-crowned night-heron, and glossy ibis. Mute swans, Canada geese, and several duck species are also abundant. During winter and migration, other common waterfowl are the gadwall, pintail, teals, American wigeon, ring-necked duck, canvasback, scaups, common goldeneye, bufflehead, old-squaw, common eider, scooters, and mergansers.

Ospreys and a few northern harriers nest along the shore. During fall migration, hundreds of American kestrels, sharp-shinned and cooper's hawks, and a few merlins and perigrine falcons migrate past Griswold Point on Long Island Sound. In winter, Essex and Haddam Neck are favorite spots for bald eagles to sit in the trees and hunt for fish and waterfowl. As elsewhere, the shoreline population of eagles and ospreys has increased dramatically since the banning of the pesticide DDT.

Rails hide in the marshes, and migrating plovers and sandpipers gather by the thousands in May and July through September to feed on the mud flats at low tide or rest in the salt marshes at high tide. Herring and great black-backed gulls are always present. In summer, common and least terns fish and nest along the inlets and beaches. Fish crows are also likely to be found here. Marsh wrens are in the cattails, and there are two species of sparrow that are found only in the sedge marshes: the sharp-tailed and the seaside sparrow.

Camping on the River

It is important to realize that most of the shoreline and islands of the River are privately owned. Under no circumstances should anyone use private property to camp, picnic, or obtain access without *first* getting permission of the owner. Be pleasant. Good manners will help open the way. Remember that if you do not obtain permission, you are liable for charges of trespassing and vandalism. In general, landowners will grant permission if they are assured that you will take care of their property.

Always leave your campsite immaculate. That way, the next time you or someone else requests permission to camp there will not be a problem. Only public landings and established campsites are mentioned in this book, although there are many areas that are suitable for camping if permission is obtained from the owner. Always contact park managers to make advance reservations in order to avoid unhappy surprises during your trip.

Here are a few guidelines to follow when camping on the River:

1 You *must* carry out what you carry in. Not only does common sense dictate that you leave the site clean for the next person, but also littering is prohibited by law.

2 Use public bathroom facilities at established campgrounds or shoreline communities whenever possible. In remote areas, bury personal waste at least 100 feet from the River's edge.

3 Use portable stoves instead of building fires (which are illegal in some areas). This leaves the ground cover undisturbed and reduces the risk of forest fires.

4 Always use biodegradable soaps.

5 Since most of the River and tributaries are not potable, always be sure to take along plenty of drinking water.

6 Do not cut vegetation or dig holes along the shore or engage in other activities that might cause bank erosion.

There are many people who boat, canoe, fish, and swim in the Connecticut River. An effort by each individual to be responsible for his own activities will result in a significant contribution in keeping the Connecticut River clean and enjoyable. The River's ecosystem is fragile and relies upon your care for its survival.

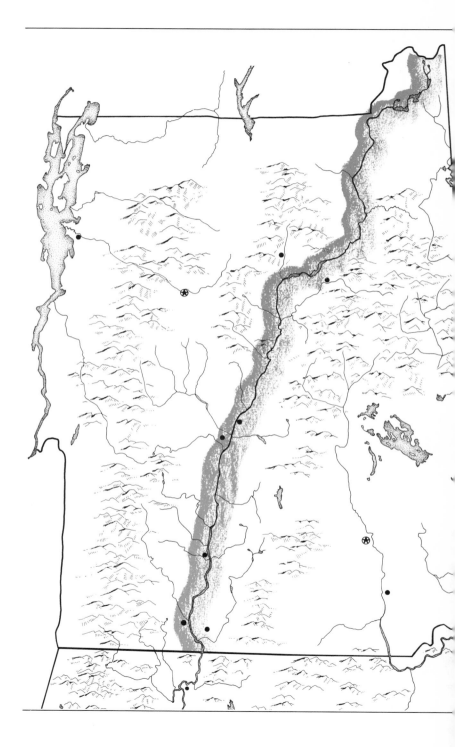

New Hampshire and Vermont

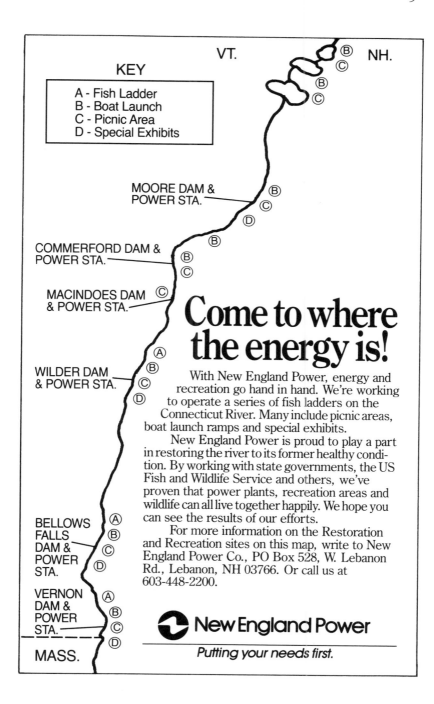

Access Areas in New Hampshire and Vermont

[408]   *Third Connecticut Lake; Pittsburg, NH;*
             ramp, parking.

[404]   *Moose Falls; Pittsburg, NH;*
             camping, fireplaces, picnic tables.

[401]   *Second Connecticut Lake; Pittsburg, NH;*
             fireplaces, picnic tables.

[398]   *Second Connecticut Lake; Pittsburg, NH;*
             fireplaces, picnic tables.

[392]   *First Connecticut Lake; Pittsburg, NH.*

[381]   *Lake Francis State Park; Pittsburg, NH;*
             camping, fireplaces, picnic tables; (603) 538-6965.

[380]   *Lake Francis State Boat Ramp; Pittsburg, NH;*
             picnic tables.

[376]   *Indian Stream School; Indian Stream, NH;*
             camping.

[369]   *Canaan, VT; just below Rte. 114 bridge.*

[355.5]   *Colebrook, NH, Rte. 26 bridge.*

[342.5]   *Lyman Falls Dam.*

[339]   *Nulhegan River; NH side.*

[320]   *Guildhall / Northumberland Dam; VT side.*

[288]   *Rte. 18 bridge.*

[286]   *Moore Reservoir; Lower Waterford, VT;*
             ramp, picnic area.

[285]   *Moore Reservoir; Littleton, NH;*
             ramp, picnic area.

[281] *Pine Grove Launching Area; Comerford Reservoir;
Lower Waterford, VT; ramp, picnic area.*

[281] *Comerford Dam; NH side.*

[274] *McIndoes Falls Dam; Monroe, NH; picnic area.*

[271] *Ryegate Dam; East Ryegate, VT; below dam.*

[265] *Woodsville, NH; below bridge.*

[260] *Bradford, VT.*

[254.5] *State Ramp; Newbury, VT.*

[251.5] *Bedell Bridge State Park; picnic area.*

[238] *State Ramp; Fairlee, VT.*

[238] *Town ramp; Orford, NH.*

[235.5] *The Pastures Campground; Orford, NH; (603)353-4579,
dock, camping.*

[229] *Wilder Lake Camping Area; Lyme, NH; (603) 353-9881,
camping, ramp, dock.*

[228.5] *State Ramp; North Thetford, VT.*

[221] *Ompompanoosuc River State Ramp; East Thetford, VT;
off Rte. 5.*

[220] *Town Ramp; Hanover, NH; dock, picnic area.*

[214.5] *Ledyard Canoe Club; Hanover, NH; boat rentals,
water, ramp, dock, rest rooms.*

[213] *New England Power Co. Landing; Wilder, VT;
picnic area.*

[212] *West Lebanon, NH; off Rte. 10.*

[211.5] *Riverpoint Park; White River Junction, VT; picnic area.*

[203.5]   *New England Power Co. Landing; Sumner Falls, VT.*

[198]   *State Boat Ramp; Cornish, NH.*

[194]   *North Star Canoe Rentals; Cornish, NH;*
           (603) 542-5802.

[193]   *Wilgus State Park; Ascutney, VT; (802) 674-5422;*
           camping, water, rest rooms.

[188]   *Claremont, NH; ramp off Rte. 12A.*

[185]   *Springfield, VT.*

[180.5]   *State Ramp; below Cheshire Bridge.*

[178]   *New England Power Co., picnic area.*

[175]   *Herricks Cove.*

[172.5]   *New England Power Co., picnic area.*

[169.5]   *New England Power Co., picnic area.*

[152.5]   *Putney, VT.*

[144.5]   *West River Marina; Brattleboro, VT; (802) 257-7563.*

[143.5]   *Brattleboro, VT.*

[143]   *Hinsdale, NH.*

[142]   *Vernon, VT.*

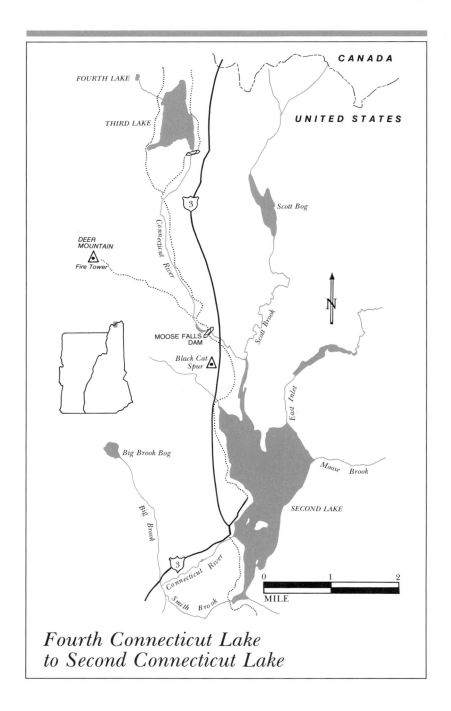

Fourth Connecticut Lake
to Second Connecticut Lake

Fourth Connecticut Lake
to Second Connecticut Lake

MILE:	410-400 (10.0 miles).
NAVIGABLE BY:	Kayak, canoe, small powerboats and sailboats on the lakes.
DIFFICULTY:	Class II-VI, depending on flow conditions; flat water on lakes.
PORTAGES:	Mile 410; Fourth Lake to Third Lake; 1/2 mile.
	Mile 408.5; Third Lake to Second Lake; 4 miles.
	Mile 400; Second Lake to First Lake; 2 miles.
CAMPING:	No established sites.
USGS:	Second Connecticut Lake 15.

The Connecticut River begins in the clouds that surround the mountains of Canada and New Hampshire. Falling rain creates tiny rivulets that join in a hollow among the spruce and fir trees and fill the Fourth Connecticut Lake just 200 yards on the American side of the U.S./Canada border. This little lake is the recognized source of the Connecticut River, which over its 410-mile length flows through four states and empties into the Atlantic Ocean at Long Island Sound.

To reach the Fourth Connecticut Lake, you must go by foot. Start at the U.S. Customs House on Rte. 3 at the Quebec/New Hampshire border. Notify the customs officer that you plan to hike into the lake via the "slash border." Hike for 3/4 of a mile, up three steep rises, to where the border bends to the right. Here you should see a large orange-and-black sign pointing left. The 1/2 mile trail to the lake passes through rough terrain and is not well marked, so stay close to the blazes. The lake itself is about 120 yards long and quite wild. You are more likely to see a moose or beaver here than another party of hikers.

You will again have to walk to go from the Fourth Connecticut Lake to the Third Connecticut Lake. It is a steep descent in places, and there is no formal trail, so stay very close to the River so as not to lose your way. The nascent Connecticut River between the two lakes is an excellent trout stream but not well suited for navigation. Here, you can say without exaggeration, that you jumped across the Connecticut River in a single bound.

The light brown waters of the Third Connecticut Lake reach a maximum depth of about 100 feet. It is a good place to look for birds and other animals, and the trout fishing is excellent. The Third Lake can be reached by car via Rte. 3. There is a boat ramp at the northern end of the lake. The length of the lake has been increased to about 1 mile by the construction of a dam at its southern end.

■ *DANGER: Unfortunately, the river between the Third Connecticut Lake and the Second Connecticut Lake is impassable in open boats. Expert kayakers can attempt this stretch of the river under certain flow conditions.* Do not *run this section until you have scouted out every inch, and don't run it in a group of fewer than three boats. This is an exceptionally treacherous stretch of river: Use extreme caution.*

The Second Connecticut Lake has also been enlarged to about 4 miles in length by the building of a dam. The River exits on the west side about 3 miles down, just past two islands.

SOURCE TO THE SEA—
A TRIP DOWN
THE CONNECTICUT RIVER

The Connecticut River has been a highway through the lands of central New England since the earliest times. There is no record, however, of anyone traveling from the highest source of the Connecticut River—Fourth Connecticut Lake—to Long Island Sound until the trip was undertaken in 1959 by a group led by the president of The Connecticut River Watershed Council, Dr. Joseph G. Davidson.

The Davidsons made the trip in seven days by canoe, powerboat, and car to "preach the gospel of conservation at every stop."

On the first day of the journey their party hiked into Fourth Connecticut Lake where Dr. Davidson filled "a jug of clear sparkling water, the kind which leaves the source of the Connecticut in its long voyage to the sea." They all had a drink of the water and Dr. Davidson noted sadly that this was "the last drink we'll take from the Connecticut." From Camp Idlewild on Second Connecticut Lake the party drove to Groveton, NH, then paddled by canoe to Guildhall, VT, where they were greeted by Vermont Governor Robert T. Stafford. From there they continued by boat and automobile to Hanover, NH, and the Wilder Dam.

From Wilder, riding in a turbojet-propelled boat, Dr. Davidson and his wife were taken down through the Hartland Rapids (Sumner Falls), where they came to grief. The boat hit a submerged rock. The travelers, however, were unhurt and transferred to other transportation for the trip to Charlestown, NH. Dr. Davidson was later reminded by a friend that it was at these same rapids that Major Rogers and his Rangers had had troubles on their journey from St. Francis, Quebec, to Fort No. 4 at Charlestown.

The Davidsons continued their trip, visiting schools, flood-control projects, pollution-control projects, and recreational sites along the River. In Bellows Falls, VT, they were greeted by a band and a parade and were treated to a steamboat ride to Brattleboro, VT.

Continuing into Massachusetts, they visited the fish lift at Holyoke Dam that had assisted 15,000 shad upriver the previous year.

The Davidsons completed the trip from West Springfield, MA, to Long Island Sound in a day. They viewed bank erosion, visited the historic Windsor Locks, and met with Connecticut Lieut. Governor John Dempsey and other state officials on this final, eventful day.

At the end of the trip Dr. Davidson displayed the two jugs of water he had collected: the clear water collected at the Fourth Connecticut Lake and another—obviously polluted—jugful collected from farther downstream. He spoke of the River as being a treasure that had become an open sewer and recalled donning a gas mask at several beautiful but odiferous locations on the trip downstream.

Dr. Davidson's mission was to raise the consciousness of the public and of the responsible officials to both the beauty of and the damage to the Connecticut River. In this he was successful ◆

Dr. and Mrs. Davidson at the Fourth Connecticut Lake.

CRWC Activities in New Hampshire

■ The Council has worked with the state legislature to establish a protective program for the watershed in New Hampshire. This would protect land, provide recreation, and provide access to the River.

■ The Council has provided funds to support research by graduate students and others on river ecology and related subjects.

■ The Council conducts canoe trips for the public on the Connecticut lakes and the Connecticut River and its tributaries.

■ The Council has worked to protect the last free-flowing reach of the Connecticut River at Sumner Falls from hydroelectric development.

■ Through its Conservancy Program the Council has protected lands that include forestland, important wildlife habitats, parks, and islands in the Connecticut River.

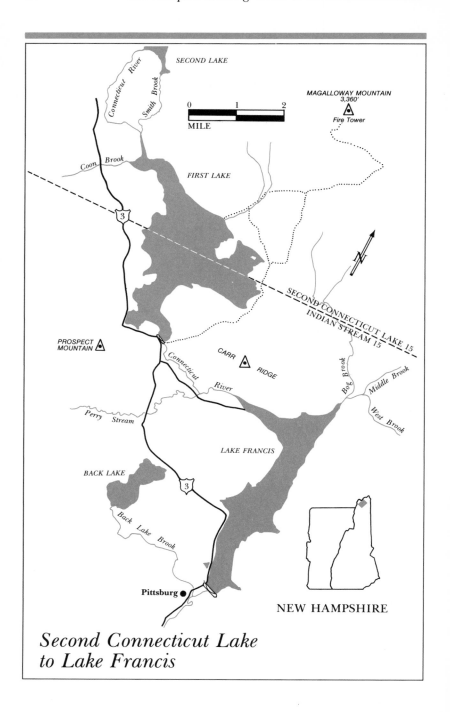

SECOND LAKE

Connecticut River

Smith Brook

MAGALLOWAY MOUNTAIN
3,360'
Fire Tower

0   1   2
MILE

Coon Brook

FIRST LAKE

3

N

PROSPECT
MOUNTAIN

SECOND CONNECTICUT LAKE 15
INDIAN STREAM 15

Connecticut River

CARR RIDGE

Bog Brook

Middle Brook

West Brook

Perry Stream

LAKE FRANCIS

BACK LAKE

3

Back Lake Brook

Pittsburg ●

NEW HAMPSHIRE

*Second Connecticut Lake
to Lake Francis*

Second Connecticut Lake to Lake Francis

MILE:	400-381 (19.0 miles).
NAVIGABLE BY:	Kayak, canoe, small powerboats and sailboats on the lakes.
DIFFICULTY:	Class II-VI, depending on flow conditions; flat water on lakes.
PORTAGES:	Mile 400; Second Lake to First Lake; 2 miles. Mile 395; First Lake to Lake Francis; 2 miles.
CAMPING:	Mile 384; Lake Francis State Park. Pittsburg, NH; (603) 538-6965.
USGS:	Second Connecticut Lake 15, Indian Stream 15.

DANGER: *In the 3 miles between the Second Connecticut Lake and the First Connecticut Lake, the River drops almost 200 feet! This section of the River should not be run except by experts in covered boats. Even so, you will have to take out and portage around several waterfalls. Don't run this section without meticulous scouting. There is no cut trail between the lakes, so you will have to bushwack or go by way of Rte. 3.*

The First Connecticut Lake is about 5 miles long and much deeper than any of the other lakes. For a bird's-eye view of the area, you can hike from the lake or the dam up Magalloway Mountain to the fire tower on top. It is a 16-mile round trip from Rte. 3, so leave plenty of time. The lake is controlled by a dam owned by the New England Power Company. Daily water-release schedules are published in the Colebrook paper. Be sure to check the schedules or call New England Power Company at (603) 448-2200. You may also write to the power company at P.O. Box 528, Lebanon, NH 03766.

■ *DANGER: The River between the First Lake and Lake Francis should be attempted only by experts in covered boats, and only when water is* not *being released.*

The first mile below the dam is likely to be steep and bumpy, followed by a mile of easy rapids until Perry Stream enters on the right. Generally, easy rapids continue for the next mile to Lake Francis. The last ³/₄ of a mile, however, contains a big drop that is *not* easy. In medium to high water, you could be in for a rough ride.

Lake Francis was created in 1940 when the state of New Hampshire built a 100-foot-high dam just north of the town of Pittsburg. (Pittsburg's town lines encompass 300 square miles, making it the largest town in New England.) The lake is about 5 miles long and covers what used to be one of the twistiest sections of the upper River. The portage around the Lake Francis Dam begins at an access area just above the dam on the north side of the lake.

Second Connecticut Lake.

ACID PRECIPITATION

One could argue that the true source of the Connecticut River is not in the lakes, streams, and bogs of New England but in the clouds above them. Rain and snow fall across the landscape and trickle through the soil, forming the countless streams and brooks that feed the Connecticut River.

Today's precipitation is not the same as the precipitation that historically has fed the Connecticut River and its tributaries. Today's precipitation is much more acidic than it was in the past.

Most experts agree that the primary cause of the increased acidity of our precipitation is industrial air pollution. Sulphur emissions become sulfuric acid when they combine with water; nitrous oxide becomes nitric acid. The burning of coal for electric power is a major source of sulphur; automobile and truck exhausts are a major source of nitrous oxide. The transformation of sulphur and nitrous oxide occurs in the atmosphere, and the acids then fall to earth as rain, snow, etc.

In some areas there is enough natural buffering in the soil to neutralize these acids. In New England, particularly at high elevations, this is frequently not the case. Where conditions are acidic, aluminum in the bedrock is released into the watertable, and generally it is this aluminum that proves toxic to fish and other species in the food chain. The waters of many lakes and streams have become so acidic that they can no longer support fish or other life.

There may be effects on the forests of the region too. Some scientists have cited dieback of trees at high elevation as being related to acid precipitation. There is also evidence that the sugar maple is susceptible to the effects of acid precipitation.

There is a scientific consensus that acid precipitation is a problem not only for the northeastern United States but also for the whole planet. The international scale of the problem has made solutions especially difficult. However, the United States and Canada have agreed to study the problem and work together for a solution ◆

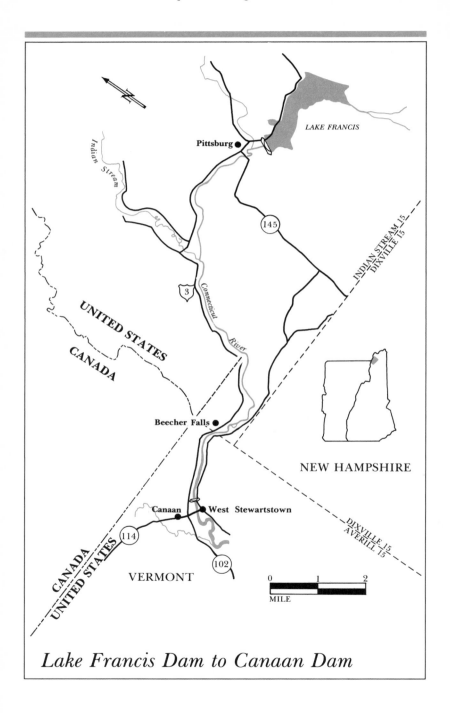

Lake Francis Dam to Canaan Dam

Lake Francis Dam to Canaan Dam

MILE:	381-368 (13.0 miles).
NAVIGABLE BY:	Kayak, canoe.
DIFFICULTY:	Class I-III.
PORTAGES:	Mile 368; Canaan Dam; west side; ½ mile.
CAMPING:	No established sites.
USGS:	Indian Stream 15, Averill 15.

Put in at the covered bridge [378] or where Indian Stream [376] comes in.

■ *DANGER: The section from below the dam to Indian Stream may be impassable when the dam is releasing water.*

From Indian Stream down to Beecher Falls is generally Class I water, although in midsummer low water could make things scratchy. Beecher Falls is usually Class II, but can increase to Class III after a heavy rain. The best passage through the falls is usually on either side. Novices will want to line down or portage. Whatever you choose, make your decision based on knowledge: *Scout it out.*

For those continuing downstream, the portage around the dam is on the Vermont side. Follow a paved road for about ½ mile to just below the bridge on Rte. 114.

A SHORT-LIVED INDEPENDENT REPUBLIC

The uppermost part of the River near the Canadian border was long the subject of border disputes between the newly formed United States and Canada. Ignoring both, the 300 or more settlers in the area set up their own Indian Stream Republic, framing a constitution and electing a president. Both Canada and New Hampshire unsuccessfully sent armed militia into the area. In 1836, New Hampshire finally took control, disbanding the republic and setting up the township of Pittsburg. The border dispute between the United States and Canada was finally put to rest in 1842 when the Webster-Ashburton treaty established the definitive line ◆

CRWC Activities in Vermont

■ The Council has worked with other organizations to protect the Ottauquechee River from pollution resulting from intense development along its headwaters.

■ The Council has protected lands that are important for agriculture, forestry, wildlife, and fisheries.

■ The Council has developed a greenway management plan for the Ottauquechee River.

■ The Council has worked with state agencies and the legislature to establish strong protection for the state's upland streams.

■ The Council conducts canoe trips to increase public awareness of the River and its tributaries and the issues facing them.

■ The Council monitors and participates in Act 250 and other regulatory processes to protect the River and lands in the watershed from inappropriate development.

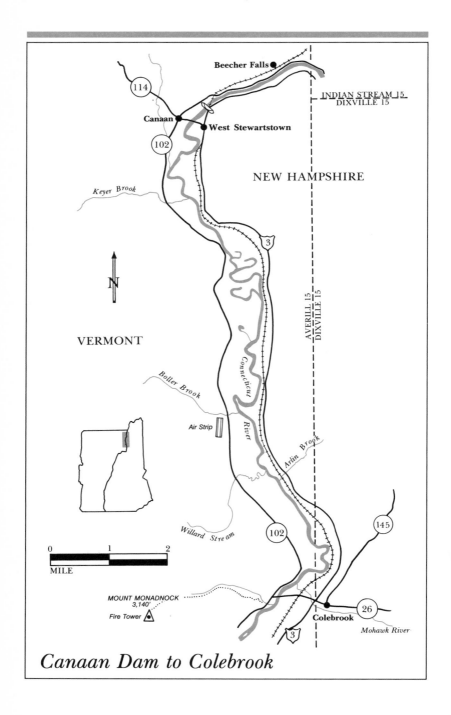

Canaan Dam to Colebrook

Canaan Dam to Colebrook

MILE:	368-355.5 (12.5 miles).
NAVIGABLE BY:	Kayak, canoe.
DIFFICULTY:	Class I-II.
PORTAGES:	None.
CAMPING:	No established sites.
USGS:	Averill 15, Dixville 15.

Below the put-in at the Rte. 114 bridge there are a few riffles before the River starts several miles of meanders. There are lots of nice sandy-point bars here that make good picnicing spots. Vermont's Mt. Monadnock looms in the distance, rising 3,140 feet. The water is generally Class I through the meanders, although July and August can see low water. For fun you can take a side trip into one of the four oxbows in this section of the River. Near Mt. Monadnock, strong winds are often channeled down the valley, making paddling difficult. Fresh water can be obtained from the rest stop on Rte. 3 just above Arlin Brook [359].

Just above the Colebrook Bridge, Rte. 26 [355.5], is a very small and informal canoe access site. From here you can walk across to the Vermont side and reach the 2.4-mile trail up Mt. Monadnock. You will get a great view of the valley from the fire tower. It is a good hike, so leave three hours for the round trip. About one third of the way up is a very pretty waterfall that makes a good snacking spot.

During the 19th century much of this area was logged for pulpwood and lumber. Great rafts of timber were floated down the River to mills as far south as Holyoke, MA.

NATURAL-VALLEY FLOOD STORAGE

The broad, flat 12,000-acre floodplain that stretches from West Stewartstown to Lancaster, NH, plays a vital role in protecting downstream cities and towns from floodwaters. All of the flood-plains and wetlands of the Connecticut River watershed function as natural-valley flood-storage areas. The largest of these is the 20,000-acre area extending from Windsor Locks to Middletown, CT. During floods, the water spills over a wide area, dissipating the destructive force of the current and depositing nutrients in the soil. Some of the water soaks into the ground, and the rest is temporarily stored until the floodwaters recede. The effect of natural-valley flood storage is to reduce the flood peak (the highest water level) as it progresses downstream. Reducing the peak reduces the destructive force of the flood and helps keep water out of the downtown areas of cities like Springfield, MA, and Hartford, CT.

In addition to the natural-valley flood storage, the U.S. Army Corps of Engineers has constructed 16 flood-control reservoirs on various tributaries in the watershed. However, it is interesting to note that the flood-storage capacity of the two major natural-valley storage areas in Massachusetts and Connecticut is 50 percent greater than the combined capacity of the 16 reservoirs. The importance of these natural-valley storage areas in protecting downstream communities cannot be overstated.

Over the last 100 years, some of this storage capacity has been lost, and more is being lost today. The most dramatic loss is from the construction of dikes that keep the floodwaters out of the floodplains. In this case, the water that otherwise would have spread across the floodplain must either move to adjacent areas—causing higher water levels there—or move on with the peak, causing increased flooding downstream. Filling in of the floodplain to raise structures above the flood level has the same effect. Paving over floodplains for parking lots and roads reduces the capacity of these areas to hold the water by preventing it from soaking into the ground. The water runs off more quickly, increasing the destructiveness of the flood and raising the peak level. The preservation of the natural-valley flood-storage areas is of critical importance in reducing the flood hazards throughout the watershed ◆

*Natural valley flood storage at Rocky Hill
and Glastonbury, CT 1984.*

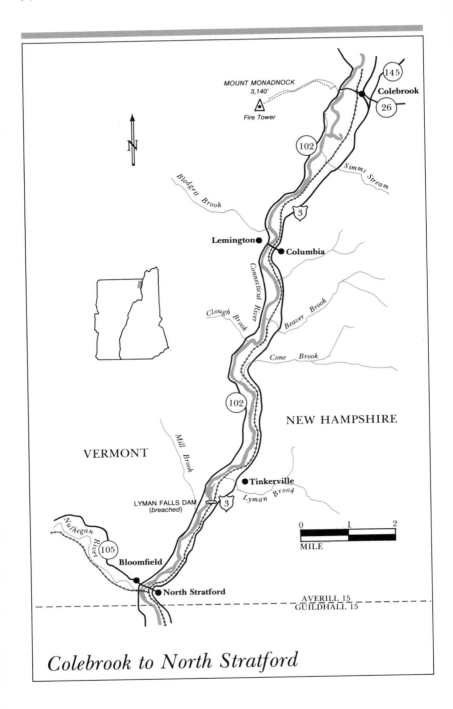

Colebrook to North Stratford

Colebrook to North Stratford

MILE:	355.5-339.5 (16.0 miles).
NAVIGABLE BY:	Kayak, canoe.
DIFFICULTY:	Class I-II.
PORTAGES:	Mile 342.5; Lyman Falls Dam (breached); Vermont side; 1/4 mile.
CAMPING:	No established sites.
USGS:	Averill 15.

Intermittent smooth water and easy rapids characterize the River between Colebrook and the covered bridge at Columbia [350.5]. Below the covered bridge there is flat water for about 2 miles followed by intermittent Class II rapids for the next 7 miles to North Stratford. From the Columbia Bridge to Lyman Falls a wilderness of scrub and trees lies close to the bank. The vegetation limits views of the wooded hills and green fields beyond but harbors a great variety of bird life.

■ *DANGER: The approach to Lyman Falls and Lyman Dam is dangerous because rapids extend all the way to the dam, and there are no good warnings that a dam is ahead. Keep close track of your position, and look well ahead. When you see a number of log crib piers in the middle of the channel, head quickly toward the Vermont shore and scout what lies ahead. The breached Lyman Falls Dam [342.5] can offer fun whitewater for the experienced paddler. However, numerous hazards must be watched for, including some steel rods sticking up out of the dam. The rapids above and below the dam are among the longest whitewater runs remaining on the Connecticut River. Don't plan on running the dam unless you are prepared to swim. In seasonally high or low water, portaging may be required.*

The three miles below the Lyman Dam is a "catch and release only" fly fishing area. After the dam, watch out for a number of boulders in the middle of the channel. From here on, there is mostly swift water, with some riffles to North Stratford, NH.

LOG DRIVES
ON THE RIVER

Deforestation in the British Isles had long been a problem for the British navy, which needed large trees for the masts and spars of its ships. The establishment of the American colonies provided a temporary answer to the problem, as the British navy had exclusive right to the tall white pine trees. The navy marked the trees with a symbol, and anyone found cutting a marked tree was severely punished.

However, the ousting of the British and the clearing of southern New England for farmland did not satisfy the demand for lumber. Trees from farther and farther north had to be cut and transported south. The easiest way to accomplish this was to float them down the Connecticut River. It was thought to be a rash idea to pass 60-foot-long logs through the Bellows Falls Gorge and other obstructions, but around 1879 the first major log drive brought down 3 million board feet of lumber to the mills in Massachusetts. Later drives would bring down 50 million board feet.

Log driving was a hazardous occupation. It began shortly after the ice went out while there was plenty of water in the River. Each year lives were lost on the drives, especially in dislodging the logjams. Some jams had to be picked apart by men balanced on floating logs. Other jams were so complete that they had to be blasted apart with dynamite. In later years, less tangle-prone 4-foot lengths were driven down the River. The drives arrived in Turner's Falls in August, having come perhaps 150 miles downstream over a three- to four-month period.

French Canadian loggers near Charlestown, NH,
circa 1900.

Breaking up a log jam.

The first major mill was at Riverside in Gill, MA. Other mills were established at Turner's Falls and Holyoke. At Holyoke a natural setback in the River made an ideal holding area for the logs and was the southernmost point of the log drives. By the 1880's the Holyoke area was one of the nation's leading producers of paper products.

The development of the railroads and highways spelled the end of the River log drives. Trucks and trains were able to transport the logs more quickly and less expensively. The last log drive on the Connecticut River was in 1930 ◆

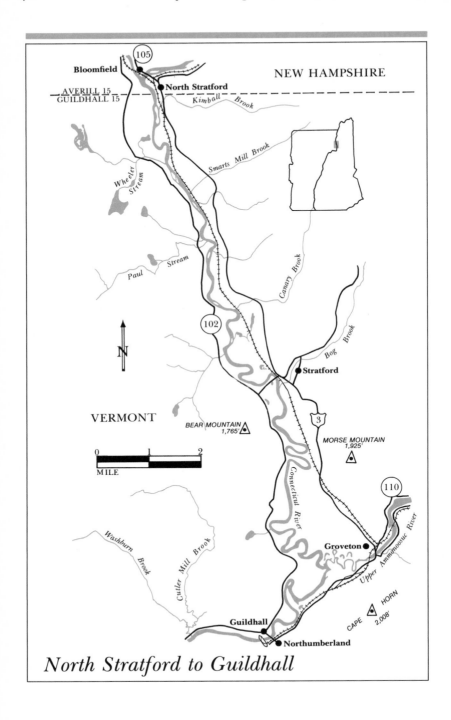

North Stratford to Guildhall

North Stratford to Guildhall

MILE:	339.5-320 (19.5 miles).
NAVIGABLE BY:	Kayak, canoe.
DIFFICULTY:	Class I; quick water.
PORTAGES:	Mile 320; Northumberland Dam (breached); Vermont side; ¼ mile.
CAMPING:	No established sites.
USGS:	Averill 15, Guildhall 15.

At the North Stratford Rte. 105 bridge [339.5], stay close to the Vermont shore to avoid the rocks and shallow water. North Stratford is a good place to stop if you are in need of supplies. (A number of houses stood in the floodplain just below the bridge until they were destroyed by ice flows in 1979.)

The Nulhegan River flows into the Connecticut from Vermont just below the bridge. There is an informal access to the River ½ mile below the bridge on the New Hampshire bank. About 1 mile below the bridge is a pitch known as the "Horse Race" where the water is fast but not difficult. Flat water in wide meanders follows the Horse Race. A glacial esker can be seen on the Vermont shore; its bare sandy slope towers about 100 feet above the River. From here to Guildhall you will wander through mile after mile of meanders, passing many oxbows, sandy-point bars, and beaches. High banks often hide the adjacent fields. The Paul Stream enters from New Hampshire at mile 333.5.

The Maine Central Railroad bridge appears 2 miles farther down [331.5], and the Stratford, NH, to Maidstone, VT, bridge is reached after another 4 miles. Near Guildhall, the Upper Ammonoosuc River enters at mile 323. From here you can see the Presidential Range of the White Mountains in the east.

■ *DANGER: The Northumberland Dam [320] is breached and poses a danger since it is not marked. Be careful at the approach, since the current can be swift. Do not attempt to run the breached dam.*

Portage the dam on the Vermont side by pulling up on the rocky bank. Carry up the bank and cross the highway. Continue down the other side of the highway, following the edge of the woods. Once at the River's edge, bear right along the channel. Put back in at the sandy beach just below the dam.

THE GREAT FLOODS

Great floods in the watershed have resulted from excessive rainfall, runoff from snowmelt, and a combination of the two. The impacts of these floods were widespread and helped spur Congress to fund flood-control projects throughout the valley.

November 1927: This flood ". . . was the greatest disaster in the history of our beautiful state," declared Vermont Governor John E. Weeks. It was estimated that a cubic mile of the Atlantic Ocean had been transported by a stream of oceanic air and dumped on Vermont's hills and valleys. All Vermont rainfall records were broken. Fifteen inches of rain may have fallen on the mountains. In the Connecticut River Valley, the White River watershed at White River Junction and the Passumpsic River Valley at St. Johnsbury were hit particularly hard.

March 1936: This New England-wide event was the result of heavy rainfall and a thaw that melted the blanket of snow and ice that covered the region. Taken together, the rainfall and the spring freshet were equivalent to 16 inches of rainfall in northern parts of the watershed. Ice jams destroyed bridges throughout the valley and caused a diversion of water across low meadowlands near Holyoke, MA. At one point the dam at Vernon, VT, was threatened by large ice flows and water that crested 10 or 11 feet over the top of the dam. A small crew of utility workers and citizens worked all night sandbagging and shoring up the dam until the floodwaters receded. The River rose 28.7 feet in Springfield and 37.6 feet in Hartford.

State Capitol Building, Hartford, CT, 1936.

September 1938: The great New England hurricane blasted up the Connecticut River Valley, causing more damage and loss of life than had any other natural event in New England's history. The death toll was greater than 600, and property damage totaled $387 million. Flooding was greatest in the tributary watersheds of Massachusetts, Vermont, and New Hampshire, though the greatest damage occurred outside the watershed along the Rhode Island coast.

August 1955: Hurricanes Connie and Diane caused the most recent widespread flooding in southern New England. After a preliminary soaking by Connie, Diane let loose with 19.75 inches of rain at Westfield, MA, an all-time record for New England. Damage was also extensive in Winsted and Farmington, CT ◆

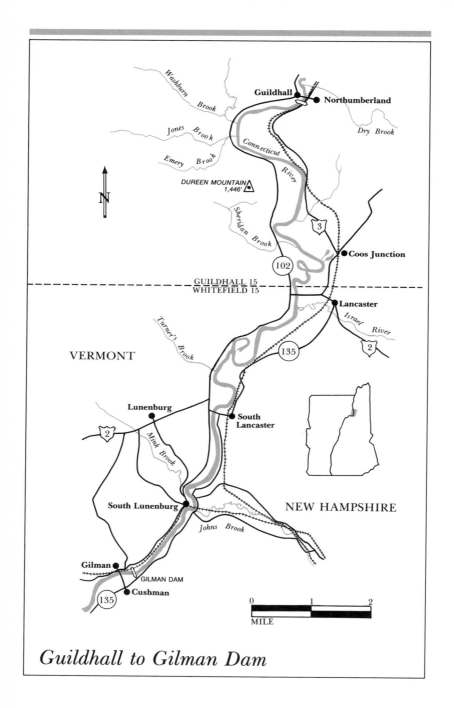

Guildhall to Gilman Dam

Guildhall to Gilman Dam

MILE:	320-300 (20.0 miles).
NAVIGABLE BY:	Kayak, canoe.
DIFFICULTY:	Class I; quick water.
PORTAGES:	Mile 300; Gilman Dam; New Hampshire side; ¼ mile.
CAMPING:	Mile 312; Prospect View Campground; Lancaster, NH; (603) 788-4960 or 788-2978.
USGS:	Guildhall 15, Whitefield 15.

To run the River below the Northumberland Dam, you will have to carry your boats from the highway, along the edge of the woods to the River. Bear right, and put in at the sandy beach just below the dam. This section of the River makes for pleasant canoeing. It is flat and meanders in wide loops, creating many oxbow lakes. There are excellent views of Mt. Washington and the Presidential Range of the White Mountains.

Six miles down from the Northumberland Dam is the covered bridge at South Lancaster and Lunenburg [314]. Another 3 miles will bring you to the railroad bridge and the Johns Brook at South Lunenburg [311]. The Johns and Israel rivers were named for the Gline brothers, the first white men known to have wintered along the banks of those rivers. In this area the Connecticut is flat, quick water, or Class I paddling. There is frequently a stiff headwind near Gilman. The Georgia-Pacific paper mill is located on the Vermont side, just north of the Gilman Dam.

The portage around the dam begins in a small cove above the dam on the New Hampshire side. Exercise caution when putting in below the dam since high water here can be dangerous.

THE COOS COUNTRY

At Guildhall the River enters into the Coos Country, an old Indian name meaning "the place of the curved river." The Coos Country extends some 100 miles south to White River Junction. This rich valley of fertile meadows and gently rolling hills edged by the White Mountains in the east and the Green Mountains in the west is often called "The Garden of New England."

The region is also known for the amount of lumber it has produced. The Kilkenny Railroad, which ran from the Kilkenny Mountain Range through the town of Lancaster, NH, carried 200 million board feet of lumber in the ten years between 1887 and 1897.

During Labor Day weekend, the Coos and Essex Agricultural County Fair is held in the town of Lancaster, NH. This old-fashioned spectacle features agricultural and livestock exhibits, horse and oxen pulling contests, and all the other activities of a good New England country fair.

On the western slopes of the White Mountains the town of Littleton, NH, is the commercial center of Coos Country. Today, Littleton is a prosperous community. However, its peak was reached in the middle of the 19th century when it was a center of the Merino sheep-raising industry. In 1840 there were 617,390 sheep in New Hampshire and 1,681,819 sheep in Vermont, or roughly 2.25 sheep per person in New Hampshire, and 5.75 sheep per person in Vermont ◆

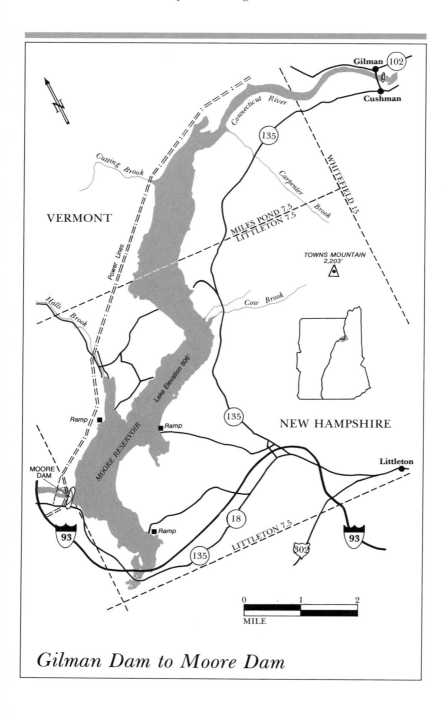

Gilman Dam to Moore Dam

Gilman Dam to Moore Dam

MILE:	300-288 (12.0 miles).
NAVIGABLE BY:	Kayak, canoe; small powerboats and sailboats on reservoir.
DIFFICULTY:	Class I, flat water.
PORTAGES:	Mile 288; Moore Dam; Vermont side; ½ mile.
CAMPING:	Mile 290; Crazy Horse Campground, Littleton, NH: (603) 444-2204.
USGS:	Whitefield 15, Littleton 15, Miles Pond 7.5, Littleton 7.5.

Swift water below the Gilman Dam requires caution while embarking and may even require moving farther downstream before putting in. After passing under the highway bridge, the River bends to the left. Riffles and rocks characterize the section of the River just before entering the headwaters of Moore Reservoir. The 1-mile-wide and 10-mile long Moore Reservoir, along with its southern partner, Comerford Reservoir, inundated what used to be Fifteen Mile Falls, through which the River dropped 350 feet over boulders and ledges.

Because of the length, width, and depth of the reservoir, strong winds and waves can cause considerable difficulty for the paddler. For this reason, it is best to paddle the reservoir in the morning when the winds are calmest. With almost no shoreline development, the scenery is spectacular. The New England Power Company has built four boat ramps—one in Vermont and three in New Hampshire—with six adjoining picnic areas. The picnic areas have tables, fireplaces, and toilets, but camping is not allowed.

To portage Moore Dam, take out on the Vermont side just above the dam.

THE MOORE RESERVOIR

Prior to the construction of the Moore and Comerford hydro-electric power dams, the section of the Connecticiut River from Gilman, VT, to the base of the Comerford Dam was known as "Fifteen Mile Falls." Cascading among the glacially deposited boulders, the River dropped almost 350 feet.

The 3,500-acre Moore Reservoir floods the falls. Behind the dam the water is 140 feet deep. The water intake valve for the power plant is 19 feet in diameter and causes water-level fluctuations of about 20 feet.

The reservoir is a popular area with boaters, and the scenery is beautiful. Yet beneath the surface, Moore Reservoir is in trouble. Plagued by water-quality problems since its construction, the reservoir is a virtual biological desert below a depth of 10 feet. The problem is a thick layer of organic sediment on the bottom of the lake discharged by the paper mill at Groteon, NH, and municipalities upstream prior to the installation of wastewater-treatment facilities. The decomposition of these organic sediments creates a biochemical oxygen demand (BOD) that uses all of the available oxygen in the water, leaving no oxygen for fish or plants. This problem is compounded during the summer months by a layer of warm water on the surface of the reservoir that does not mix with the cooler, denser water down below. During the summer, oxygen from the surface never replenishes the oxygen used by the decomposing organic sediments on the bottom. The result is a total lack of oxygen below the surface layer and no place for the fish to go: The surface water is too warm, and there is nothing to breathe down below.

The problem is slowly being rectified by the construction of sewage-treatment plants and the installation of new wastewater-treatment equipment at the Groteon mill that will remove two-thirds of the BOD it generates. Though it may take some time for the accumulated sediments on the bottom to decompose, Moore Reservoir may one day be able to support year-round fish populations ◆

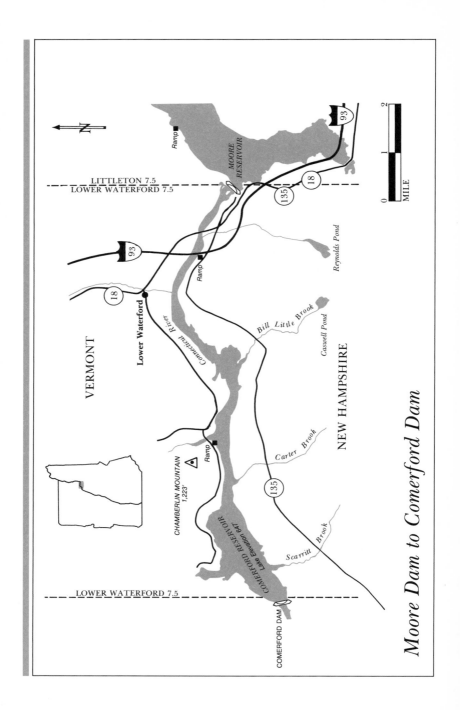

Moore Dam to Comerford Dam

Moore Dam to Comerford Dam

MILE: 288-281 (7.0 miles).
NAVIGABLE BY: Kayak, canoe, powerboats, and sailboats.
DIFFICULTY: Flat water.
PORTAGES: Mile 281; Comerford Dam; New Hampshire side; ½ mile.
CAMPING: No established sites.
USGS: Lower Waterford 7.5.

If you are looking for an access point from the highway, there is a good spot to put in under the Rte. 18 bridge on the New Hampshire side just below Moore Dam. Standing 178 feet high, Moore Dam is the largest hydroelectric power station on the Connecticut River. The I-93 overpass is prominent just below the power plant. This entire section of the River is the headwaters of the Comerford Reservoir and hence flat-water paddling with little current. Strong winds on the reservoir can present a problem, so the easiest paddling will be in the morning. This attractive and undeveloped area is owned by the New England Power Company. The company maintains a boat ramp on the Vermont side.

The approach to Comerford Dam (the second highest on the River, standing 170 feet) is well marked. There is a picnic spot at the dam on the New Hampshire side, and it is from here that the portage around the dam begins.

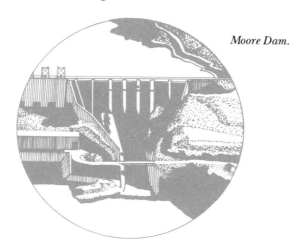

Moore Dam.

THE WHITE MOUNTAINS

Between Moore and Comerford dams one can see the Presidential Range of the White Mountains in the east. Mt. Washington, the highest peak in the Northeast, reaches 6,288 feet. The other peaks of the Presidential Range are Mt. Jefferson, 5,725 feet; Mt. Adams, 5,805; and Mt. Madison, 5,363 feet. The White Mountains are geologically different from the Green Mountains and the rest of the Appalachians. The White Mountains are the eroded roots of ancient volcanoes. Early explorers sailing along the New England coast could, on a clear day, make out the snow-covered summits, leading to their being called the White Hills, or White Mountains.

Providing little opportunity for farming and forming a barrier to travel, these mountains offered little incentive to settle in the area. In the 19th century the valleys and peaks of the White Mountains yielded a rich harvest of logs for the building and industrialization of America. The stripping of the forests exacted a heavy environmental price. Fierce fires and destructive floods followed the cutting of the forests.

In 1911 Congress passed the Weeks Act, sponsored by a native of Lancaster, NH, and authorizing the purchase of land to establish national forests, particularly in the eastern part of the country. One of the first national forests to be established was in the White Mountains. Today the land is managed under a multiple-use mandate. Timber products, water-resource protection, and recreation are the primary uses of the White Mountain National Forest ◆

Rabbit Hill Inn

*Lower Waterford,
VT 05848
(802) 748-5168*

An early 19th-century inn of
unique charm in Vermont's most-
photographed village, nestled in the
upper Connecticut River valley and
overlooking the majestic White
Mountains of New Hampshire.
Good food and wine, comfortable
rooms, some with fireplaces and all
with private bath. Canoeing, nature
trails, bird watching, mountain
climbing, fishing, sailing, cross-
country skiing, golf, tennis,
antiquing, summer theatre all
nearby. On route 18 near the river
between Saint Johnsbury, VT and
Littleton, N.H.

Your hosts, The Charlton Family

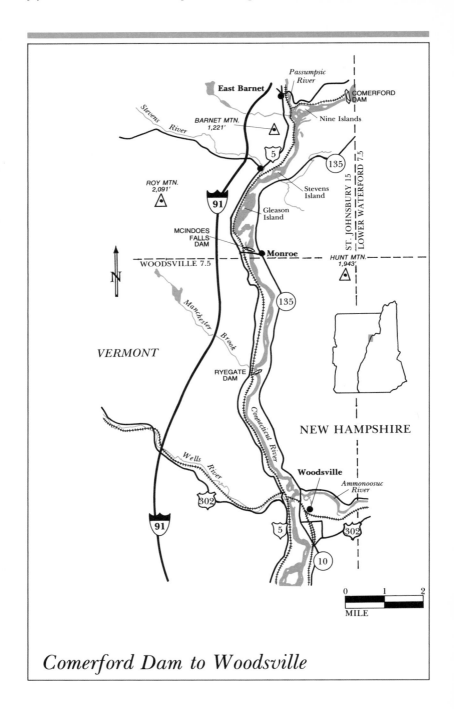

Comerford Dam to Woodsville

Comerford Dam to Woodsville

MILE:	281-265 (16.0 miles).
NAVIGABLE BY:	Kayak, canoe.
DIFFICULTY:	Class I-III, depending on flow.
PORTAGES:	Mile 274; McIndoes Falls Dam; New Hampshire side; 200 yards.
	Mile 271.5; Ryegate Dam; New Hampshire side; 1/4 mile.
CAMPING:	Mile 266; Saddle Island; CRWC (603) 643-5672.
USGS:	Lower Waterford 7.5, St. Johnsbury 15, Woodsville 7.5 or 15.

DANGER: *The canoeing from Comerford Dam to McIndoes Falls is considered by many to be the most challenging on the Connecticut River. This also means that it can be very dangerous, especially if the Comerford Station is operating near capacity, thus making the River swift. The water level of the River can fluctuate up to 6 feet, depending on the amount of water being released from the dam. DO NOT CAMP on any island or near the bank in this stretch of the River. In the past, the sudden rise in the water level has swept campers away.*

About 1 mile down from the dam there are a number of boulders in the streambed that you should take care to avoid. In another mile, the Passumpsic River [279] enters from Vermont, slightly increasing the current. Stevens Brook enters at Barnet [277], and a highway bridge crosses the River soon thereafter. From here to McIndoes Falls, the River is wide and shallow; the best course is usually on the Vermont side.

Watch for the "Portage" signs on the New Hampshire side as you approach McIndoes Falls Dam [274]. There is a picnic site just below the dam. From here it is 2.5 miles to Ryegate Dam.

■ *DANGER: The approach to Ryegate Dam [271.5] is not marked. Look for the sharp bend in the River from right to left, and listen for the roar of the falls as warning that you are coming up on the dam. You may also be able to see the smokestack of the mill at the dam. Stick very close to the New Hampshire side and take out right after the bend to avoid being swept over Ryegate.*

The portage trail begins across from a grassy area and goes through some woods and over a few slippery rocks, terminating at an open area below the dam. (At the time of this writing, the installation of a hydroelectric power plant at the dam has been proposed and may affect the approach and portage in days to come.) If you are starting at this point, the access site can be reached by car on the Vermont shore 150 yards beyond the paper mill from a parking lot near the shore.

On summer weekends you may have trouble on the section of the River below Ryegate due to insufficient water. During the week water is released by the mill and the generating stations upstream, and hence there is more water in the River. Conditions can be muddy for about a mile below the dam. The rest of this section is easy Class I paddling. Much of the River in this stretch is bordered by cornfields, most of which cannot be seen because of high banks. During the summer you may scrape on the cobblestone-like bottom when you get within 1 mile of Woodsville, where the River bends toward New Hampshire. To avoid scraping, keep close to the Vermont shore. In higher water, this stretch is Class I/II paddling. Cliffs rise above the banks on either side. The fishing here is quite good.

After turning the bend [266], you will see an island (two islands during high water) called Saddle Island, owned by The Connecticut River Watershed Council. The island makes a good camping spot (permission to camp is not required). Just beyond the island, where the River bends toward Vermont, there can be turbulent standing waves where the Ammonoosuc River enters from New Hampshire and the Wells River from Vermont.

CAUTION: In spring it is best to scout this area from shore because of the volume of water and the size of the standing waves. It is better to be smart than soaked . . . or worse. The best course is usually on the Vermont side.

THE STEAMBOAT *BARNET*

The little town of Barnet, VT, lent its name to a small steamboat that was built in 1826 to prove that River navigation between Hartford, CT, and points upstream was possible and that a proposed canal from New Haven, CT, to Northampton, MA, was not needed. The steamboat was named for the town of Barnet because just north of the town lay Fifteen Mile Falls, which was considered an impassable barrier.

The 75-foot-long, 14.5-foot-wide *Barnet* left Hartford on November 11, 1826, and failed to climb the Enfield Rapids on the first attempt. A second attempt was made two days later after its machinery was "strengthened," a scow lashed to either side, and 30 poling men recruited. That afternoon the *Barnet*'s arrival in Springfield, MA, caused such a commotion that the courthouse was emptied of all the spectators.

The *Barnet* was then pulled over Williamansett Falls, steamed through the South Hadley bypass, and reached Bellows Falls without incident. Unfortunately, the hope of reaching Barnet came to a disappointing end when the *Barnet* proved too wide to fit through the locks at Bellows Falls. However, by traveling 125 miles north of Hartford and climbing 200 feet, the *Barnet* proved that upstream navigation on the Connecticut River was possible.

The *Barnet*'s return to Hartford was signaled by the firing of a cannon and was greeted with much enthusiasm, except, of course, by the backers of the New Haven-to-Northampton canal. Three years later the *Barnet* was one of the first boats to go through the newly opened Windsor Locks Canal around the Enfield Rapids ◆

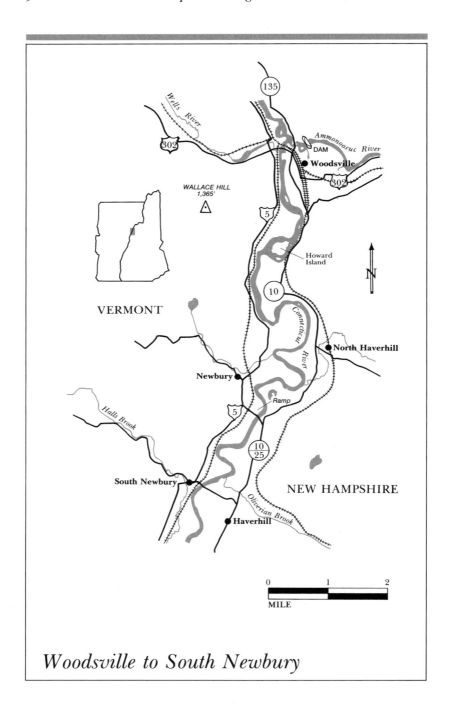

Woodsville to South Newbury

Woodsville to South Newbury

MILE:	265-251.5 (13.5 miles).
NAVIGABLE BY:	Kayak, canoe.
DIFFICULTY:	Class I-II.
PORTAGES:	None.
CAMPING:	No established sites.
USGS:	Woodsville 15.

Immediately below the bridge at Woodsville is a side road paralleling the River on the New Hampshire shore. There is an access site at a sandy beach off this road. The River narrows through a gap right below Woodsville and becomes Class II paddling for a short period. Occasional ripples may be encountered until reaching Howard Island [263.5], which is quite large and wooded. Passage on the New Hampshire side is recommended because of shallow water on the Vermont side. Very large meanders follow. The water is flat and has very little flow. The deeper water will usually be found beneath the steepest bank or on the outside of the curve. Most of the surrounding area is farmland.

The flat water backed up behind Wilder Dam begins at a sharp left sweep of the River at Placey Farm. This is one of the most photographed spots along the River. You may want to get out and climb up to Route 5 to look at the view, including the beautifully maintained Placey Farm. The fishing is quite good in the quiet waters down to the Newbury access ramp. The most frequently taken fish are largemouth bass, then smallmouths, and sometimes a walleye. If you head up a side stream, you may catch a rainbow trout. Just above the Newbury bridge [254.5] is an access ramp maintained by the state of Vermont.

Take note of the streambank stabilization project on the New Hampshire side just below the bridge. Various materials are being experimented with to help protect floodplain agricultural land from erosion, a problem aggravated by the cutting of streambank trees.

You can paddle up Oliverian Brook [252] to do some birding or fishing. It is narrow, shallow, and enclosed by vegetation: perfect for birds. After Oliverian Brook there is a cement pillar sticking out of the riverbed marking the site of the old Bedell Covered Bridge [251.5], which was destroyed in a windstorm following a hurricane two months after it was reconstructed in 1979.

MAJOR ROBERT ROGERS AND THE RANGERS

Major Robert Rogers and 200 Rangers were sent out by British General Jeffrey Amherst to revenge the capture by the St. Francis Indians of two officers traveling under a flag of truce. (The flag was actually a ruse to get past French patrols, but that didn't seem to bother Amherst.) Rogers set out by boat from Crown Point on the southern end of Lake Champlain in New York. Since the French controlled most of the lake, the Rangers had to travel at night. By the time they reached the northern end of the lake, 59 men had to be sent back because of injury or illness. Rogers then hid his boats and supplies, leaving a small watch party, and headed on foot through the wilderness to the Saint Lawrence River.

Unfortunately, the French discovered his trail and sent 200 men in pursuit. It was at this time that Rogers sent word to Amherst to send supplies from Fort No. 4, up the Connecticut River to the Wells River, "that being the way I shall return, if at all. . . ."

Rogers attacked the Indian village of St. Francis at 3 a.m. on October 6, 1759, killing, he believed, 200 Indians. (The actual count was closer to 30.) Taking whatever supplies they could, the Rangers immediately headed back south, with more French and Indians in hot pursuit.

After two weeks of freezing temperatures and no supplies, Rogers' small band finally reached the Wells River only to find the still warm embers of the fire left by the rescue party that had fled, thinking Rogers' group were Indians. Said Rogers, "Our distress on this occasion was truly inexpressible."

Rogers and three Rangers then headed down the Connecticut River on a timber raft, promising to return with provisions within ten days. Rogers lost the raft—and nearly his life—in the rapids at White River Falls. Since they had no axes, they made a second raft by burning trees to the right length. They nearly lost their lives a second time at Sumner Falls. Rogers reached Fort No. 4 in six days. Within a half hour of his arrival at the fort, he sent supplies back north, which arrived exactly on the day promised. Of the 141 Rangers who took part in the raid on St. Francis, only 92 returned. What at the time was thought a daring and successful raid was, in fact, a reckless and costly mistake ◆

Bend in the River near Bradford, VT.

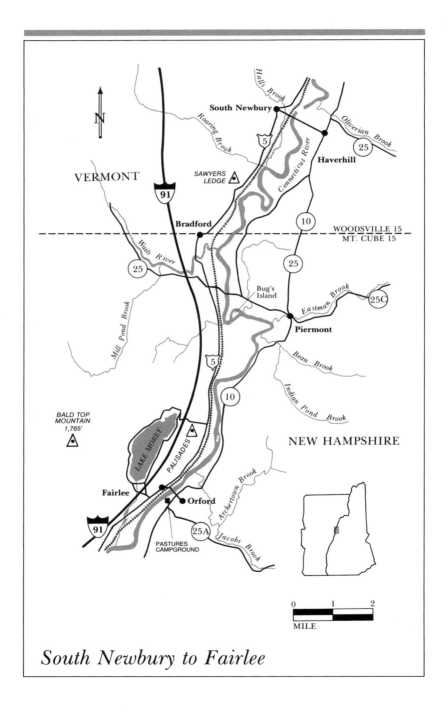

South Newbury to Fairlee

South Newbury to Fairlee

MILE: 251.5-235.5 (16.0 miles).

NAVIGABLE BY: Kayak, canoe.

DIFFICULTY: Flat water.

PORTAGES: None.

CAMPING: Mile 235.5; The Pastures; Orford, NH.
                     (603) 353-4579.

USGS: Woodsville 15,
                     Mt. Cube 15.

Two and one half to three miles downstream of South Newbury is a recent oxbow cutoff that is a good spot for fishing. The sandy shore below the cutoff is lined with agricultural fields. The current is slack due to Wilder Dam. The Waits River [245.5] is a very attractive whitewater run in the spring and early summer, as well as an excellent fishing area.

About a mile down from the Waits River confluence you will pass under the Rte. 25 bridge. About a half mile past this girder bridge the River bends sharply to the east. On the Vermont side is a very pretty brook that falls almost directly into the River. There is a good fishing spot on the opposite shore.

On the left as you go east is Bug's Island, with rock shoals on the right. You will then pass through a very large oxbow [243.2], which is a good area for spotting water birds. The subsequent stretch of River is bordered by pastureland and agricultural fields. You can occasionally catch views of some of the adjacent cliffs such as "The Palisades" in the west, a formation of Fairlee granite. Just below the Fairlee/Orford Bridge [235.5] is the Pastures Campground in New Hampshire.

This is a good spot to take out. A small dock on the left side is the only landmark. On this stretch of River, in 1792, Samuel Morey of Orford successfully ran a steamboat between Orford and Fairlee 15 years before Robert Fulton launched his steamboat.

Take some time to walk through Orford, especially down the line of beautiful Federal houses know as "Bullfinch Row." There is also a good access area in Orford just south of the campground. You can pick up supplies or have a bite to eat in either Orford or Fairlee.

ORFORD'S RIDGE HOUSES

In the 1830's Orford, NH, was a prosperous community with a population of about 1,800—roughly three times its present population. Washington Irving visited the town and wrote, "In all my travels in this country and Europe, I have never seen any village more beautiful than this. It is a charming place; nature has done her utmost here."

The seven Federal style houses on the ridge above the Connecticut River are often called "Bulfinch Row" because they were thought to have been designed by the famous architect Charles Bulfinch. The Wheeler house, built in 1816, may have been designed by Asher Benjamin, an associate of Bulfinch, but the rest of the houses were designed by local craftsmen.

The first house on the ridge was built by Obadiah Noble in 1773 and was bought by Samuel Morey of steamboat fame in 1799. Morey made extensive renovations to the house, bringing it to its present appearance in 1804. It was here that Morey built and patented an internal combustion engine in 1826. In an attempt to prove that it could propel a carriage, Morey attached the engine to a wagon, which was propelled so quickly that it crashed into the wall of the workshop.

The other houses were built by local bankers, lawyers, and merchants. The last house on the ridge was built by Stedham Willard in 1839 and was apparently designed to rival the home of his father-in-law and next-door neighbor, Mr. Wheeler ◆

Wheeler House, Orford, NH.

A participating inn in *Canoe Vermont!*

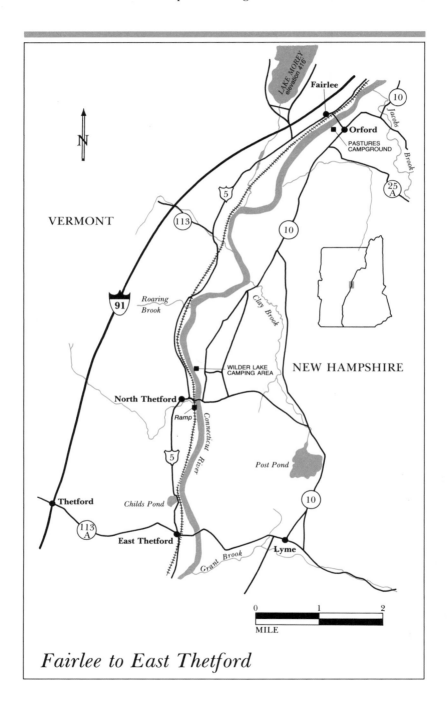

Fairlee to East Thetford

Fairlee to East Thetford

MILE:	235.5-226 (9.5 miles).
NAVIGABLE BY:	Kayak, canoe.
DIFFICULTY:	Quick water, flat water.
PORTAGES:	None.
CAMPING:	Mile 235; The Pastures Campground; Orford, NH; (603) 353-4579.
	Mile 229; Wilder Lake Camping Area; Lyme, NH; (603) 353-9881.
USGS:	Mt. Cube 15.

The trip downstream to East Thetford begins at the Fairlee/Orford Bridge. Rich agricultural lands, especially cornfields, border this section of the River. Both slow water and strong headwinds can make paddling difficult. About 4 miles below Orford, Clay Brook [231.5] comes in from New Hampshire. You can paddle up this scenic tributary to reach a good birding area just beyond a covered bridge.

Wilder Lake Camping Area [229] on the New Hampshire bank of the River maintains excellent launch and camping sites with some facilities.

At North Thetford [228.5] the remains of an old bridge are prominent. There is a take-out spot on the west side with a ramp maintained by the Vermont Department of Fish and Wildlife. No formal access sites are available between North Thetford and East Thetford.

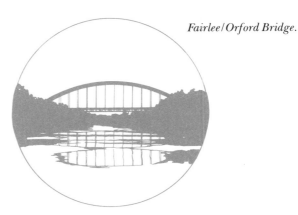

Fairlee/Orford Bridge.

THE FIRST STEAMBOAT?

When travelers on the Connecticut River go under the bridge between Fairlee, VT, and Orford, NH, they pass the house of Samuel Morey, the inventor of one of the first successful steamboats and the inventor of an internal combustion engine that predated Duryea's automobile engine.

The encyclopedias all say, however, that Robert Fulton invented the first successful American steamboat. Local tradition has it that Morey deserves the credit. The full story is somewhat more complicated.

One of the keys to success in steam navigation was the use of the side paddle wheels, which Morey used in a public demonstration in 1797. Through an oversight, Morey did not patent their use. Fulton, however, did in 1811, and from that time Morey could not legally use them.

Morey had turned his attention to improving the steam engine and applying it to the purpose of propelling boats as early as 1790. Morey described his steamboat as "about 19 feet long, 5½ [feet] wide, and the engine occupies only about 18 inches of the stern, and sometimes goes between seven and eight miles per hour. . . ."

In order to avoid an audience, Morey first tried out the dugout steamboat on a Sunday, when everyone was supposed to be in church. However, a few hookey players witnessed the launching from the New Hampshire shore. The boat ran with a paddle wheel at the bow and made about 4 miles an hour steaming upriver. The next time Morey ran his steamboat, the whole town came out to watch.

Fulton probably knew of Morey's invention. During his summers in New York, Morey made contact with Chancellor Robert Livingston and interested him in his steamboat work. In 1797 he took Livingston on one of his boats, and Livingston promised Morey a "considerable sum" if he could make the boat go 8 miles an hour. Livingston also offered Morey $7,000 for the right to use his invention on the lower section of the Hudson River, but Morey turned him down. In June Morey exhibited a side-wheel steamboat in Philadelphia. At some point the two men visited each other at their respective homes, but no agreement was ever reached.

In 1801 Livingston went to Paris, France, and met Robert Fulton. Soon afterward the two men were granted a monopoly on steam navigation in New York State. They began work on a steamboat design, and in 1807 Fulton's steamboat made her historic voyage up the Hudson River, propelled by side paddle wheels.

Morey was a native of Hebron, CT, who, in 1766, at the age of three years, came with his family to Orford by ox sled. The last 60 miles of the trip were made on the frozen Connecticut River because the Indian trail north of Charlestown, NH, was too narrow for the sled.

Morey's other engineering accomplishments included building the canal—locks, inclined planes, and dams—around the rapids in the Connecticut River at Bellows Falls, VT. In later years he moved to Fairlee, VT, where he died at the age of 80 years in 1843. In 1890 he was recognized by the Vermont Legislature when the nearby Fairlee Pond was officially named Lake Morey ◆

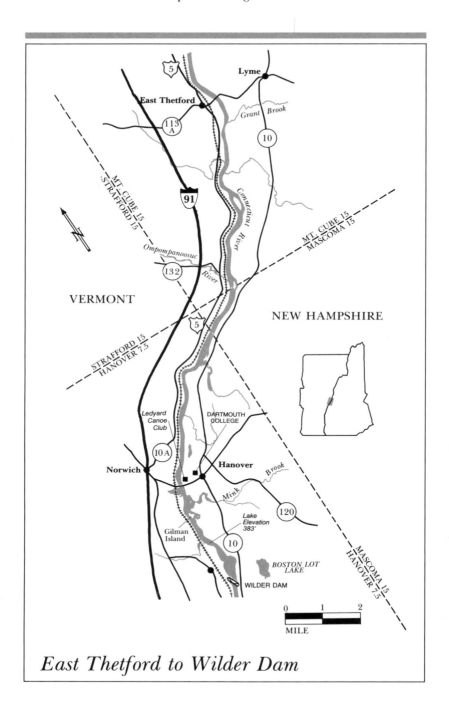

East Thetford to Wilder Dam

East Thetford to Wilder Dam

MILE:	226-212 (14.0 miles).
NAVIGABLE BY:	Kayak, canoe, powerboats, and sailboats.
DIFFICULTY:	Flat water.
PORTAGES:	Mile 212.5; Wilder Dam; 1/4 mile; east side; (802) 295-3191.
CAMPING:	Mile 217; Chieftain Motel; Hanover, NH; (603) 643-2550.
USGS:	Mt. Cube 15, Mascoma 15, Hanover 7.5.

Canoeists and kayakers can paddle up Grant Brook [225.5] on the New Hampshire side and under a bridge into a marshland for birding. Below Grant Brook on the New Hampshire side is a state wildlife protected area where birding is also good. There have been several beaver sighted in this area.

The agricultural land then gives way to a wooded shoreline. At mile 221, the Ompompanoosuc River enters from Vermont. For a nice side trip, head under the railroad bridge at the mouth of this tributary and into a fairly wide marshy area. A Vermont state landing is located beyond the railroad bridge on the Ompompanoosuc River.

The Hanover town landing and dock is located a mile below the Ompompanoosuc River. The steep and forested ridge along the New Hampshire bank a mile south of the landing is the site of a glacial esker. Part of this area is maintained by the Pine Park Association and has very nice woodland trails along the River that are good for strolling, but camping is not permitted. At Dartmouth College's Ledyard Canoe Club [214.5] in Hanover, a boat ramp, dock, and canoe rentals are available. The Dartmouth College crew races rowing shells on this part of the River during the spring and fall. If time permits, you might want to visit Dartmouth College to see its fine art collections and architecture. Hanover is also a good place to pick up supplies.

The Appalachian Trail crosses the Connecticut River at the Ledyard Bridge between Norwich and Hanover. The property on the Vermont side just south of the bridge is owned by the Montshire Museum and is the proposed site of a new natural science museum. One nature trail was opened in 1985, and others are planned.

About ½ mile south of the bridge is Gilman Island. Chambers Memorial Park, a nature area south of Gilman Island, is owned by The Connecticut River Watershed Council and also has nature trails. The New England Power Company picnic site and landing is located on the Vermont shore at mile 213. Wilder Dam is about ½ mile farther downstream. If you plan to continue your trip south of the dam, keep to the New Hampshire side and take out no closer than ¼ mile upstream from the dam.

CAUTION: Small craft should be careful of strong winds in this section, especially near the dam.

Wilder Dam was built on the site of the White River Falls—the spot where Robert Rogers and his famous Rangers saw their raft shattered during their return from a punitive expedition against the St. Francis Indians in 1759.

The New England Power Company runs a Visitors Center [(802) 295-3191] at the dam that has exhibits on the new fish ladder and other related subjects.

JOHN LEDYARD

The Ledyard Canoe Club (founded in 1920) and the Ledyard Bridge are named for John Ledyard, who has been described "for capacity of endurance, resolution, and physical vigor," as "one of the most remarkable of modern travelers."

Born in Groton, CT, in 1751, Ledyard entered Dartmouth College in 1772, with a view to fitting himself for missionary duty among the Indians. Tiring of the confining classroom, Ledyard left the college and lived among the Indians of the Six Nations for several months. Finally abandoning the idea of becoming a missionary, he embarked down the Connecticut River in a canoe of his own making and paddled down to Hartford. After a short stay he shipped out of New London as a common seaman in a vessel bound for the Mediterranean.

In the years following, Ledyard served in the British navy with distinction, accompanied Captain Cook on his third voyage around the world, and traveled extensively throughout northern Europe, Asia, and Africa. He is also credited with persuading President Jefferson to send Lewis and Clark on their famous journey to the west coast in search of trading partners and knowledge of the West. Ledyard died in Cairo, Egypt, in 1789 on the eve of an exploratory trip into the interior of the continent.

Each spring, in memory of John Ledyard, members of the Dartmouth Outing Club retrace his route down the Connecticut River by canoe ◆

THE MONTREAL EXPRESS

A few miles north of White River Junction was the scene of one of the worst train wrecks in New England's history. On the night of February 5, 1887, the last four cars of the Montreal Express derailed while crossing the bridge over the White River, resulting in 34 deaths and 49 persons injured. The cars, made of wood, fell from the bridge to the frozen river and were set afire by the wood stoves used for heat. The wooden bridge also caught fire and was destroyed. The accident attracted nationwide attention and was one of the factors responsible for the enactment of the Railway Appliance Act of 1893, the first national legislation setting safety standards for railroad equipment ◆

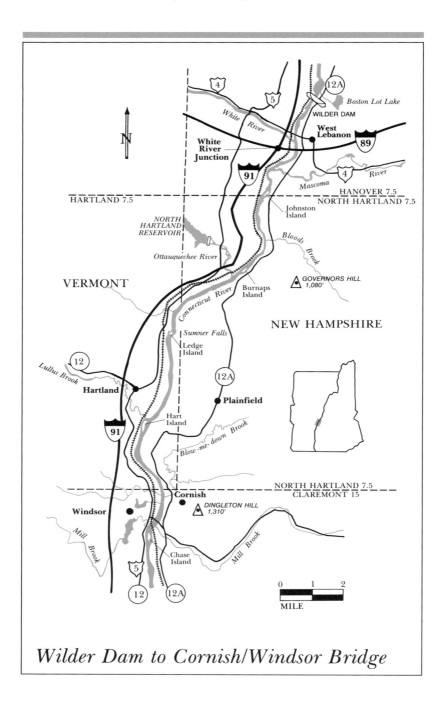

Wilder Dam to Cornish/Windsor Bridge

Wilder Dam to Cornish/Windsor Bridge

MILE: 212-197 (15.0 miles).

NAVIGABLE BY: Kayak, canoe.

DIFFICULTY: Class I-IV.

PORTAGES: Mile 204.5; Sumner Falls (Hartland Rapids);
               Vermont side; ¼ mile.

CAMPING: No established sites.

USGS: Hanover 7.5,
               North Hartland 7.5,
               Hartland 7.5.
               Claremont 15.

The portage around Wilder Dam is on the New Hampshire side. Walk along the Rte. 10 guardrail or on the bank of the River. Follow the grassy dirt road as it leads back to the River. As you approach the River, the road turns into a trail, sections of which are quite steep.

CAUTION: Releases from the dam are made without warning. Secure your boats at the put-in so they aren't swept away by a sudden rise in the water level.

The New England Power Company runs a Visitors Center [call (802) 295-3191 for information] that has exhibits on the new fish ladder and related subjects. The Visitors Center is open from Memorial Day through Labor Day. There is also a parking area with picnic tables.

The stretch from Wilder Dam to the Ottauquechee River is an isolated, pretty section with fairly swift water and riffles and a couple of small Class II rapids. Osprey, ducks, and beaver are often seen in this area, and the fishing is good.

A mile below the dam you will pass the confluence of the White River [211.5]. Because of the purity of the White River, it is considered a prime potential spawning ground for the Atlantic salmon.

CAUTION: The water at the White River confluence can be very swift.

There are picnic tables at Riverpoint Park at the confluence of the White and Connecticut rivers. After the White River enters, watch for bridge abutments. Just below the bridge, be careful of a few large boulders.

Between the White River and the Mascoma River [210.5], two municipalities discharge treated wastewater into the River.

There is an access spot behind the K-Mart Plaza on Rte. 12A. Head for the southwest corner of the lot and follow a primitive road down to the River's edge. Next you will pass under the Rte. 89 bridge. There is an active community of beaver in this area.

CAUTION: Beginners should be careful in this area as river conditions can vary widely. Boaters should expect swelling and strong winds in the spring.

Pick your path carefully through the Johnson Island [209.5] area because the flow can be quite strong when the water is high. When the water is low, you may have to walk your boats to get by. The New Hampshire Department of Fish and Game owns the land on both sides of Bloods Brook [208]. There is a nice spot to stop at the southern end of Burnaps Island.

About ¼ mile down from Burnaps, the Ottauquechee River [206.5] comes in from the west. A quarter mile up this tributary is a covered bridge, a waterfall, and a power plant next to it that belongs to the White Current Corporation. The North Hartland Flood Control Reservoir [(802) 295-2855] is another mile upstream. There is a hydroelectric power plant at the 150-foot-high dam, which is operated by the Vermont Generation and Transmission Cooperative [(802) 635-2331]. While visitors are not welcome at the plant, there are picnic facilities at the flood-control area.

Just below the Ottauquechee, take care to avoid the huge boulders known as "Hen and Chicken Rocks." Downstream from these rocks, as the River becomes wider and shallower, you will have to pick your way carefully to keep from scraping bottom.

■ *DANGER: Two signs reading "Danger—Falls Ahead" are located about ½ mile above Sumner Falls on the Vermont side. The falls are also known as Hartland Rapids. Listen for the roar of the water as a warning, although in low water it may not be loud enough to be heard. Lives have been lost at this dangerous location.*

Pull toward the Vermont bank as the River bends toward New Hampshire and proceed cautiously to a rocky outcropping with a portage sign. Walk along the rocks for 50 to 75 yards up an incline to the short trail that enters the woods and leads to a dirt road. A picnic area is established at this junction.

Bear left on the road that goes downhill to a beach at a cove. This road can be reached from Rte. 5, although it is difficult to find. Whirlpools and a fast current necessitate caution when leaving the cove. Do not paddle back up to the falls because of the dangerous backflow.

Following the rapids, the channel is mostly straight with moderate flow between steep banks. In this isolated area, Mt. Ascutney, the highest peak in the Connecticut River Valley, dominates the view to Hart Island [201.5]. Watch for rocks and riffles on the New Hampshire side of the island. Sandpits along the Vermont shore mark the site of an esker. Steep banks in this region limit views.

Blow-me-down Brook enters from the east at mile 198.5. Between the brook and the covered bridge is a New Hampshire state access site off Rte. 12A. You may want to stop here and take a side trip on foot to the Saint-Gaudens National Historic Site in Cornish [(603) 675-2175]. Also in Cornish is "The Oaks," the home and studio of painter and illustrator Maxfield Parrish (1870-1966), who was famous for his fairytale and romantic scenes, many of which were inspired by the local countryside. Cornish was a popular summer resort in the early 1900's and the site of Woodrow Wilson's summer White House in 1914 and 1915. The Cornish covered bridge will come into view at mile 197. Windsor, VT, is the site of the signing of Vermont's constitution in 1777 and a cradle of the machine-tool industry as exhibited in the American Precision Museum [(802) 674-5781].

HART ISLAND: HYDROPOWER OR FREE-FLOWING RIVER?

In one sense, the Connecticut River is really a chain of reservoirs behind hydropower dams. The dams were constructed where the energy potential of the water was at its peak: at the foot of dramatic rapids and waterfalls and in gorges. From the Holyoke Dam in Massachusetts to the dam on the Second Connecticut Lake in Pittsburg, NH—the energy in the falling water of the River has been harnessed by dams. One result is reliable and relatively inexpensive electricity. Another result is that there are only a few segments of the River that are free flowing and not flooded by dams.

One such segment extends from the base of Wilder Dam to just south of the Cornish/Windsor Bridge. Fast water, flat water, dangerous rapids at Sumner Falls, islands, good fishing, and a remarkable diversity of scenery make this stretch one of the most enjoyable on the River.

At the Hartland/Windsor town line, one encounters an island to the west. This is Hart Island. In 1970, the National Park Service identified Hart Island as a "significant site," meaning that its location, degree of protection, and uniqueness were such that its acquisition should be considered. However, hydropower developers also consider Hart Island a significant site, and have made several proposals for the construction of a dam at the island.

Each of the proposals would have flooded Sumner Falls and turned this beautiful free-flowing stretch of river into another power pool. Other effects on the valley would have been the flooding of hundreds of acres of farmland, another barrier to migrating salmon and shad, and the dramatic alteration of the area's aquatic ecosystems. Along with other organizations and residents, the CRWC has opposed the construction of a dam at Hart Island as well as all other dams across the mainstream of the Connecticut River ◆

DAMS ACROSS THE CONNECTICUT RIVER

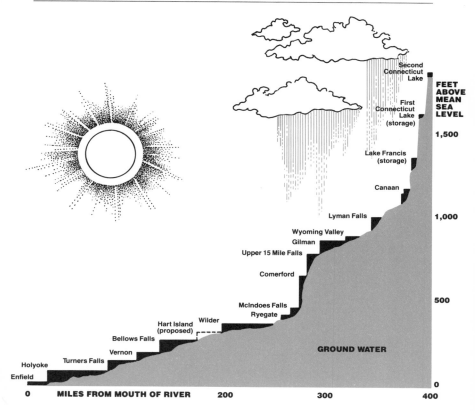

Saint-Gaudens National Historic Site

Saint-Gaudens Rd.
(off Rte. 12A)
Cornish NH 03745
603-675-2175
Mid-May–October 31; daily
8:30-4:30.
Guided tours of the home, gardens and studios of Augustus Saint-Gaudens (1848-1907), one of America's foremost sculptors.

▶ I-89 to exit 20 or I-91 to exit 8 or 9, then to Rte 12A in Cornish.

THE VERMONT STATE CRAFT CENTER

AT WINDSOR HOUSE

Main Street • P.O. Box 1777 • Windsor

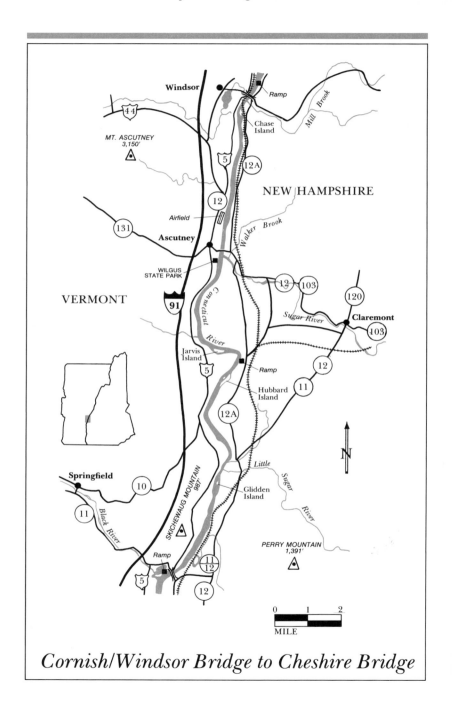

Cornish/Windsor Bridge to Cheshire Bridge

Cornish/Windsor Bridge to Cheshire Bridge

MILE:	197-180.5 (16.5 miles).
NAVIGABLE BY:	Kayak, canoe.
DIFFICULTY:	Class I, quick water.
PORTAGES:	None.
CAMPING:	Mile 194; North Star Canoe Rentals; Cornish, NH; (603) 542-5802. Mile 191.5; Wilgus State Park; Ascutney, VT; (802) 674-5422.
USGS:	Claremont 15.

Immediately following the Cornish/Windsor Bridge the two Mill brooks enter, one from the east and one from the west. The B&M Railroad Bridge is reached about ⅜ of a mile south of the covered bridge. A 5-mile-long straightaway in the River starts below Chase Island. Here the River is bordered by agricultural fields and offers many views of the Mt. Ascutney foothills. Camping is allowed with permission at mile 194 in Balloch's Crossing at North Star Canoe Rentals.

The Rtes. 12 and 103 highway bridge is at the end of the long straightaway and just north of Wilgus State Park. Both access and camping are available at the park as well as water and bathrooms.

As the River winds on, you will pass Jarvis Island [189]. Following Jarvis Island and a sharp bend toward Vermont there is a new access site with a ramp and picnic area that can be reached via Rte. 12A in Claremont, NH. Hubbard Island comes up at mile 187.5 and is a good place to look for wildlife. As you head farther south, you will pass high, sandy banks into which cliff swallows have carved their homes. There are lots of birds in the area around the confluence with the Little Sugar River. Just below the Cheshire toll bridge [180.5] is a good access area with a sloping cement ramp maintained by the state of Vermont. The ramp can be reached from Rte. 5.

SAINT-GAUDENS NATIONAL HISTORIC SITE

For River travelers who wish to stretch their legs and probe the natural history of the area as well as enjoy some cultural diversion, a visit to the Saint-Gaudens National Historic Site in Cornish, NH, is most rewarding. The park, open from May through October, is located on NH Rte. 12A, 9 miles north of Claremont, NH, and 2 miles from Windsor, VT. The superintendent's address is R.R. 2, Box 73, Cornish, NH 03745. Phone: (603) 675-2175.

The park consists of the home, gardens, and studios of Augustus Saint-Gaudens (1848-1907), one of America's greatest sculptors. There are also more than two miles of well-marked nature trails on the property. This was Saint-Gaudens' summer residence from 1885 to 1897 and his permanent home from 1900 until his death in 1907.

"Aspet," the sculptor's home, was once an inn along the stage road between Windsor, VT, and Meriden, NH. During the summer of 1883, Saint-Gaudens began remodeling the house. His furnishings are retained and reflect the character of the man and the tastes of his friends from the nearby Cornish colony of artists.

Adjacent to the house is the artist's personal studio, and nearby are the gardens and the Gallery, which house many of the sculptor's works, including a copy of his famous *The Puritan*. A short walk leads to the Ravine Studio, where Saint-Gaudens worked from time to time, and the start of the Ravine Trail, a ¼-mile walk along an old cart path that abounds with ferns and wildflowers ◆

THE CORNISH/WINDSOR BRIDGE

The first bridge from Cornish, NH, to Windsor, VT, was built in 1796 and was rebuilt three times until it was finally swept away in the flood of 1865. The Cornish/Windsor Bridge that now stands was built in 1866. Stretching 460 feet, it is the longest covered bridge in the U.S. It is a National Engineering Landmark and is listed on the National Register of Historic Places. The bridge was sturdy enough to survive the flood of 1936 and the hurricane of 1938 when many other bridges were destroyed. There are three other covered bridges in Cornish, all designed by James Tasker (1826-1903), who could neither read nor write ◆

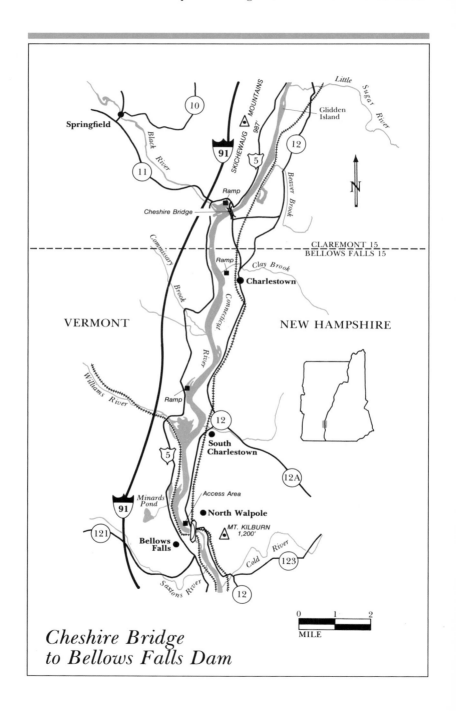

Cheshire Bridge
to Bellows Falls Dam

Cheshire Bridge to Bellows Falls Dam

MILE:	180.5-169.5 (11 miles).
NAVIGABLE BY:	Kayak, canoe.
DIFFICULTY:	Quick water.
PORTAGES:	Mile 169; Bellows Falls Dam; New Hampshire side; 1½ miles.
CAMPING:	No established sites.
USGS:	Bellows Falls 15, Claremont 15.

Just below the steel Cheshire bridge is a Vermont state access area with a cement ramp. The re-created "Fort at No. 4" stands in a field across from the confluence of the Black River and the Connecticut River [179.5] in Charlestown, NH. The original fort, built in 1745, was the northernmost English settlement in the valley at the time of its construction and played an important role in the French and Indian Wars. Camping is not permitted at the fort, but some facilities are available in the adjacent municipal picnic area. Call the fort, (603) 826-5700, for information and a schedule of events.

After the picnic area the River begins to wind through meadows. At roughly mile 178, the New England Power Company maintains a landing and picnic area on the New Hampshire side that has both a dock and a ramp. Look for the power transmission lines overhead. Just opposite Lower Meadows is another New England Power Company access area [172.5]. The Williams River enters just south of this.

As you approach Bellows Falls, the Connecticut narrows. Paddle along the New Hampshire bank until you see the take-out point at the New England Power Company access area [169.5]. Look for a small brick building just beyond a small inlet. If a vehicle-assisted carry around the Bellows Falls Dam is desired, contact Raymond Aumand in advance at (802) 445-5321.

THE FORT AT NO. 4

On a rise of ground above the Connecticut River in Charlestown, NH, the authentically re-created Fort at No. 4 gives the modern-day visitor a look into the mid-18th century, particularly the years 1740-60. Nine log houses plus the Great Chamber and Watch Tower, within a palisade of 724 pointed logs, constitute a replica of the original village of Charlestown. Costumed interpreters demonstrate the crafts of spinning, weaving, and candle making as well as the military crafts of bullet molding and musketry.

The site of the original fort is actually 3 miles south on Rte. 12, on the village Main Street, and is marked by a large boulder and a state historical sign. The reconstruction of the fort has been in progress since 1960, and its most recent building is the Lieut. Isaac Parker two-story garrison house with a huge center chimney and five fireplaces.

The fort is open from mid-May to late October. On the Fourth of July weekend, in addition to the usual craft activities, it has become a tradition to host a militia group, who, in regimental dress, present a military muster. Also in July a colonial battle reenactment has become an annual event. A smaller though similar affair in August re-creates the famous April 1747 siege when Captain Phineas Stevens and 30 men successfully repulsed a vastly superior force of French and Indians to ensure British supremacy in New England.

The canoeist or boater traveling the Connecticut River will find it worthwhile to tie up at the riverbank below the fort and take a short walk up to the fort. For more information, call (603) 826-5700 ◆

Indian Shutters Inn
1791 STAGE COACH

Excellent Dining
English Pub
Outdoor Deck
Open Seven Days

(603) 826-4445
Charlestown — on the River

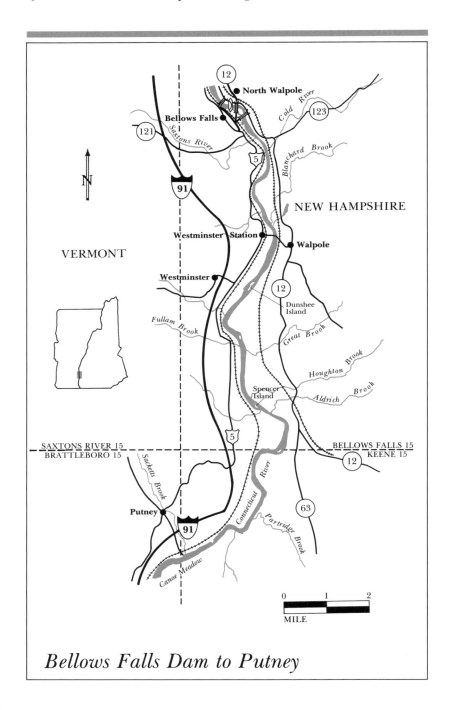

Bellows Falls Dam to Putney

Bellows Falls Dam to Putney

MILE:	169-152.5 (16.5 miles).
NAVIGABLE BY:	Kayak, canoe.
DIFFICULTY:	Quick water, flat water.
PORTAGES:	None.
CAMPING:	No established sites.
USGS:	Bellows Falls 15, Keene 15, Brattleboro 15.

From the New England Power Company landing, the portage is 1 1/2 miles along NH Rte. 12 to an access area. You can also cross the bridge from North Walpole, NH, to Bellows Falls, VT, turn left at the center of town, down past Frank Adams' Grist Mill, and put in about 1/4 mile below the mill. While in Bellows Falls you will find several things worth seeing, including Pennacook Indian carvings along the riverbank below the falls, the fish ladder, and Visitors Center at the New England Power Co. hydroelectric station, and the Bellows Falls Canal, now part of the power station. The first bridge across the Connecticut River was built at Bellows Falls in 1784 at the site of the present concrete Vilas Bridge.

After putting in, you will find quick water and flat water all the way to Putney. The canoeing is good, and the scenery is beautiful.

Across and just downstream from the access ramp the Saxtons River enters from the west. At mile 166.5, the Cold River enters from the east. In low water, keep to the Vermont shore to avoid scraping bottom in this area.

Downstream a few miles is the Rte. 123 bridge at Walpole [165]. Just after Dunshee Island [163.5] and across from Boggy Meadows is the town of Westminster, VT. New York's colonial administration held court here at the Cumberland County Courthouse. Opposition to the Court led to the "Massacre of March 13, 1775." It was also here that "New Connecticut," later Vermont, was declared an independent state on January 16, 1777.

Passing Spencer Island [159.5], you will come to a large bend at Putney Great Meadows. There is often a good selection of waterfowl to be seen near the island at the southern end of the meadows. Another 7 miles of easy paddling will bring you to Putney.

BELLOWS FALLS FIRSTS

The first bridge across the Connecticut River was built at Bellows Falls in 1785. The covered bridge was 365 feet long and 50 feet above the water. Bellows Falls can also claim one of the earliest canals in the country. The canal took ten years to build and was opened in 1802 with a dam and nine locks around the falls. The canal served as a passageway for river traffic for some 50 years. However, soon after the arrival of the railroad in 1849, river traffic disappeared and the canal came to be used only as a conduit for water power ◆

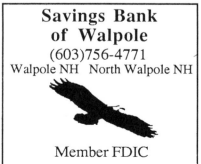

HETTY GREEN

Vermont towns are replete with all sorts of unusual characters. A longtime resident of Bellows Falls, Hetty Green (1835-1916) inherited a large fortune from her father and managed it so shrewdly that she was considered the greatest woman financier of her time. Known as the Witch of Wall Street, her shrewdness was exceeded only by her stinginess. Her refusal to pay for medical care for her son, Ned, resulted in the subsequent amputation of his leg. She left an estate of $100 million (1916 dollars!) and now rests in Immanuel Church cemetery. But she probably does not rest well, because Ned spent his fortune freely and was considered "as profligate as his mother was parsimonious" ◆

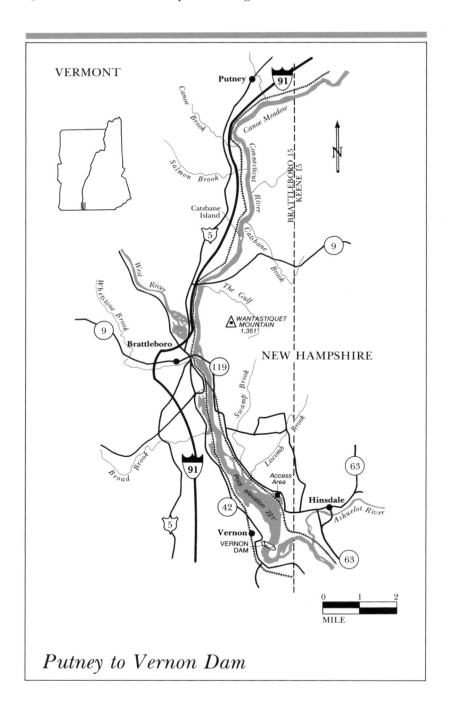

Putney to Vernon Dam

Putney to Vernon Dam

MILE:	152.5-138.5 (14.0 miles).
NAVIGABLE BY:	Kayak, canoe, sailboats, and powerboats.
DIFFICULTY:	Quick water, flat water.
PORTAGES:	Mile 138.5; Vernon Dam; west side; ¼ mile.
CAMPING:	Mile 144.5; Connecticut River Safari; Chesterfield NH; (603)363-4724.
USGS:	Brattleboro 15.

After leaving the landing at Putney, you will pass the very pretty Canoe Meadows [152] in New Hampshire. Following this is a long straightaway ending at the confluence of Catsbane Brook [148]. Catsbane Island follows, just around the bend. Two miles farther south you will come to the Rte. 9 bridge [145.5]. Right below this on the New Hampshire side is "The Gulf," a gorge that skirts the northern edge of Wantastiquet Mountain.

About another mile past the Rte. 9 bridge the West River [144.5] enters from Vermont. If you head under the railroad and highway bridges you will find many good fishing and birding spots among the islands of the West River as well as several places to put in or take out. For those with strong arms and wills, you can paddle up the West River several miles against a strong current. However, it will probably be more fun to drive 10 or 15 miles up Rte. 30 and paddle down. For the experienced boater, the West River offers some of the best whitewater in New England and has been the site of the National Canoeing Championships. Spring and early summer are best. The flow of the West River is regulated by Ball Mountain Dam in Jamaica, VT. The West Dummerston Covered Bridge across the West River is a good picnic spot, and supplies are available at a nearby variety store.

Just south of the West River is the city of Brattleboro, VT. If you are in need of supplies, you will be able to find almost anything here. Route 119 crosses the Connecticut River at Brattleboro by leapfrogging an island in the middle of the River [143.5]. At the southern end of the city is the Boston and Maine railroad bridge [142.5]. From this point to the Vernon Dam, meadows and marshlands line the River, offering refuge to fish and fowl. There are several islands in the pool area above the dam.

You may take out either at the access point under the railroad causeway in New Hampshire or portage the dam by starting at the log boom on the Vermont side. However, in the past, this take-out has been difficult because of floating logs and other flotsam and jetsam at the boom. Portage signs will lead the way. There are two picnic areas with fireplaces next to the portage trail at the Vernon Dam.

The Vermont Yankee Nuclear Power Plant has an Energy Information Center adjacent to the power plant. It is open to the public during normal business hours. Special arrangements for groups can be made by calling (802) 257-1416. Tours of the power plant itself are no longer available.

Vermont Yankee.

NUCLEAR ENERGY

The River has long been a source of energy through the physical force of falling water. This force was first used to generate mechanical power to turn wheels and power mill factories. Falling water was later used to generate electricity. Two nuclear power plants were attracted to the River, not for the power of the water but for its cooling potential.

In 1967 the Connecticut Yankee Atomic Power Company began operations in Haddam Neck with a generating capacity of 575,000 kilowatts. The Vermont Yankee Nuclear Power Plant at Vernon began generating five years later with a capacity of 545,000 kilowatts. Connecticut Yankee, operated by Northeast Utilities, is one of the leading commercial nuclear facilities in the world in terms of total power generated and reliability. After a five-year study, The Connecticut State Water Resources Board concluded that the power plant had caused little harm to the River's aquatic life.

Vermont Yankee's record has been less favorable due to early safety problems and the discharge of radioactive water into the River. The plant, however, has operated without incident for the last five or more years ◆

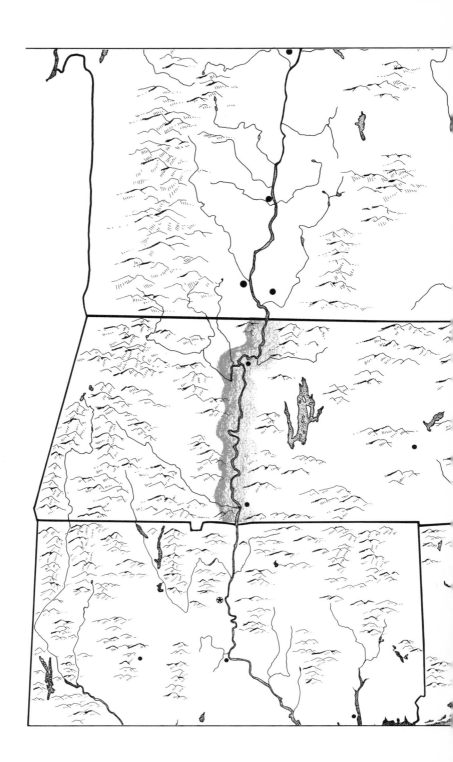

Massachusetts

Marinas, docks and access points in Massachusetts

Mile	Name	Parking	Ramp	Dock	Telephone	Water	Ice	Rest Rooms	Gasoline	Diesel Fuel	Transient Slips	Transient Moorings	Food / Hot ▼ Cold ●	Marine Supplies	Bait ▼ Tackle ●	Rent / Canoes ▼ Kayaks ●	Rent / Powerboats	Rent / Sailboats	Pump Out	Marine Railway ▼ Hoist ●	Storage
130	Pauchaug Brook State Ramp Northfield, MA	✓	✓																		
122.5	Riverview Picnic Area Northfield Farms, MA (413) 638-9300	✓																			
119	Barton Cove Gill, MA (413) 638-9300	✓	✓	✓	✓	✓	✓								▲	✓					
119	State Boat Ramp, Barton Cove Gill, MA	✓	✓																		
118	Town Ramp Turner's Falls, MA	✓	✓																		
114	Access Area, Turner's Falls, MA off Poplar St. at railroad bridge																				
106	Access Area, Sunderland, MA below Rte. 116 bridge off School St.	✓	✓																		
102	Cow Bridge Brook Boat Ramp Hatfield, MA, off Kellogg Hill Rd.	✓	✓	✓	✓	✓															
92.5	Sportsman's Marina, Hadley, MA (413) 584-7141, at Coolidge Bridge	✓	✓	✓	✓	✓					✓		✓		●						

Marinas, docks and access points in Massachusetts

Mile	Name	Parking	Ramp	Dock	Telephone	Water	Ice	Rest Rooms	Gasoline	Diesel Fuel	Transient Slips	Transient Moorings	Food / Hot ▼ Cold ●	Marine Supplies	Bait ▼ Tackle ●	Rent/ Canoes ▼ Kayaks ●	Rent/ Powerboats	Rent/ Sailboats	Pump Out	Marine Railway ▼ Holst ●	Storage
89	Mitch's Marina, South Hadley, MA (413) 584-9732, off Rte. 47	✓	✓	✓	✓	✓	✓	✓	✓	✓	✓	▲									✓
87	State Ramp, Easthampton, MA at the Oxbow off Rte. 5	✓	✓																		
87	Oxbow Marina, Northampton, MA (413) 584-2775, off Island Rd.	✓	✓	✓	✓	✓	✓	✓	✓	✓		●	●	✓	▲ ●		✓				✓
85.5	Brunelle's Marina, South Hadley, MA (413) 536-3132, off Alvord St.	✓	✓	✓	✓	✓	✓		✓												
81	Access Area, South Hadley Falls, MA 1/4 mi. below upper Rte. 116 bridge	✓	✓			✓															
79	Jones Ferry Marina, Jones Ferry Rd. Holyoke, MA (413) 533-3996	✓	✓	✓	✓	✓	✓	✓		✓		▲ ●									✓
76	State Boat Ramp, Chicopee, MA below Rte. I-90 bridge, off Granger St.	✓	✓																		
71	Bondi's Island Boat Ramp West Springfield, MA	✓																			
70.5	Riverfront Park Springfield, MA	✓																			

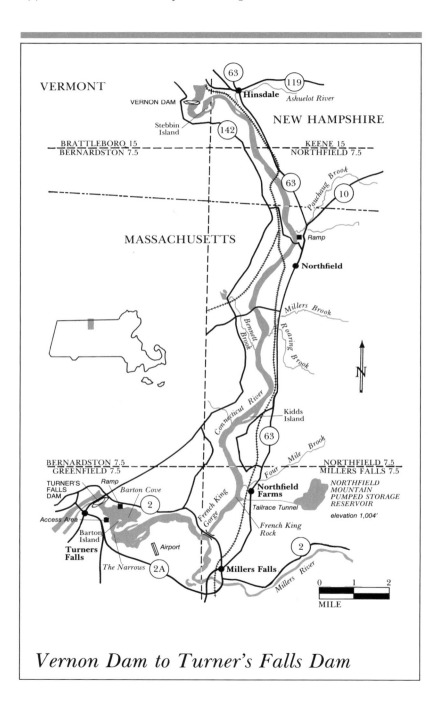

Vernon Dam to Turner's Falls Dam

Vernon Dam to Turner's Falls Dam

MILE: 138.5-117 (21.5 miles).

NAVIGABLE BY: Kayak, canoe, small powerboats on pool above Turner's Falls Dam.

DIFFICULTY: Quick water, flat water.

PORTAGES: Mile 117; Turner's Falls Dam; west side; 4 miles [See text and call Northeast Utilities at (413) 774-2221 ext. 4451 for information.]

CAMPING: Mile 125.5; Munn's Ferry; Northfield, MA

Mile 119; Barton's Cove; Turner's Falls, MA (413) 863-9300.

USGS: Brattleboro 15, Keene 15, Northfield 7.5, Millers Falls 7.5, Greenfield 7.5.

Before you head down the River, take a minute to inspect the fish ladder at the dam. It was built in 1981 to facilitate the restoration of Atlantic salmon and American shad to the upper River.

Once you embark, you will paddle through a tight curve to the left. You will be going through a small gorge and hence there will be few views of the surrounding countryside. Stebbin Island is right at the end of the turn. During times of low flow, you can paddle up the Ashuelot River [136.5] into the town of Hinsdale, NH, for supplies. Below the Ashuelot, you will pass a narrow island, and in 1 mile, go under the Boston and Maine Railroad bridge [133].

The Massachusetts state line is at mile 132. This stretch of the River below the state line is flat, open, with slow water, and five-to six-foot banks that obscure views of the adjacent fields. You can take out on the north side of the Schell Bridge [130.5] at the state's Pauchaug Brook Boat Ramp in Northfield and walk into this very attractive old town. Continuing downstream, you will go under the Boston and Maine Railroad again at mile 130.

Passing under the Bennett Meadows Bridge [128] and around a couple of gentle bends, you will find yourself at Munn's Ferry [125.5], an old River crossing. On the east bank Northeast Utilities operates a camping and picnicing area exclusively for boaters on a first-come, first-served basis. Four tent platforms, an Adirondack shelter, toilet facilities, and water are available. Just downstream is Kidds Island [125]. The best passage is on the west side.

A nice place for a picnic is Northeast Utilities' Riverview Picnic Area [122.5] in Northfield Farms near the intake/outlet for the Northfield Mountain Pumped Storage Hydroelectric Plant. From this location Northeast Utilities operates a 60-foot tour boat, the *Quinnetukut II*.

If you walk up the main road about a mile, you will come to the Recreation and Environmental Center associated with the hydroelectric facility [(413) 659-3714].

CAUTION: Immediately following Northfield Farms is French King Rock and the French King Gorge [121.5]. The Rock at the beginning of the gorge is enormous and can create turbulent water even when the rest of the River is calm. Owing to the depth of the water, most of the Rock is submerged. Pass on either side close to shore. As you enter the gorge, the current will pick up considerably.

While in the gorge, 250-foot rock walls will rise above you. In the late spring, the overhanging cliffs are full of blossoming mountain laurel. Way overhead is the French King Bridge (Rte. 2) [121].

■ *DANGER: At the southern end of the gorge, the Millers River joins the Connecticut. In medium to high water, this confluence can be very rough due to both the volume and speed of the water.*

Where the Millers River joins it, the Connecticut makes a sharp turn to the right. The steep rock walls of the gorge gradually fall away as the River widens near the Turner's Falls Dam.

Proceed onward through the Narrows and into the calm lake waters of the pool. The lake is quite deep, and the fishing is good. Northeast Utilities operates a camping area at Barton Cove that has fresh water, toilets, a picnic area, and rental equipment. For information or reservations call (413) 863-9300. Before Memorial Day call (413) 659-3714. You may want to take a peek at the Cliff and Plunge Pools in Barton's Cove. Also in the cove is a restaurant and a state boat ramp.

CAUTION: The Turner's Falls Dam and the Northfield Mountain facility create artificial "tides" of up to 3 feet. Always secure your boat while exploring on foot.

The pool is a resting and feeding area for waterfowl, gulls, and raptors (notably ospreys and bald eagles) during the spring and fall and for heron, egrets, and sandpipers during the late spring, summer, and early fall. The artificial tides create mud flats where the birds can easily find food.

Built in 1798, the original timber pier dam at Turner's Falls was the first dam on the Connecticut River. Originally built to supply water for a navigational canal around the falls, Turner's Falls Dam is now used to generate electric power.

To reach the start of the portage, keep to the left of Barton Island and head downstream to the public boat ramp on the right (north) bank upstream of the floating boat barrier at the dam. Northeast Utilities provides a free canoe portage service from the boat ramp. To avoid delays, call (413) 774-2221 ext. 4451 at least three days in advance of your planned arrival. Call again when you reach the boat ramp. Canoeists and equipment are trucked to the put-in point below Northeast Utilities' Cabot Station hydroelectric plant.

If you want to portage yourself, you should take out at the town ramp in Turner's Falls on the *west* (left side as you head down river) side of the River. Walk up First Street, which starts as a dirt road. Turn left onto Main Street and pass the Farren Hospital. Turn left again onto Greenfield Road. Turn right onto Poplar Street just before the Montague City Bridge. You can put back in below the railroad bridge. The total length of the self portage is about 3 miles. This long carry is necessary because there is no water beneath the dam except in times of flood; all the water is diverted through the canals for industrial use.

Although it is not accessible from the River, you may want to make a special trip to see the fish lift installed at the dam to help migrating fish reach their spawning grounds in the upper River.

THE NORTHFIELD MOUNTAIN PROJECT

The Northfield Mountain Pumped Storage Hydroelectric Plant, owned by Northeast Utilities, is one of several electric generating stations using the resources of the River. This facility is unique, however, because it stores the potential to produce electrical energy in addition to generating it. Electricity itself cannot be stored. Water, however, and the potential to generate electricity with it, can be moved and stored relatively easily.

Here water from the Connecticut River is pumped uphill to the top of Northfield Mountain. It is then allowed to run back down through turbines to generate electricity. Water is pumped up when electrical demand is low, usually at night or on the weekends, and the company has extra power from its other facilities. The water is stored in a reservoir near the summit of Northfield Mountain until the demand is high (perhaps in the late afternoon). Then water is released to supplement the company's generating capacity.

Northfield Mountain was selected for a pumped storage facility for several reasons. The metamorphic rock of the area is stable and provides the structural integrity needed for the tunnels and caverns. It is near the River and has a sufficient elevation to create an adequate hydrologic head to generate energy. The Turner's Falls Dam created a reservoir from which the water could be pumped and the terrain of the mountain's summit permitted the construction of an adequate storage reservoir near the top.

When the facility is operating, there are four pump/turbines that either pump water up to the storage reservoir or generate electricity from the water flowing down. When pumping, the water is drawn through the tailrace tunnel to the powerhouse. It is then pumped up through the pressure shaft to the reservoir. Each pump can pump 22,500 gallons per second. The reservoir has a capacity of about 5½ billion gallons of water. When running in reverse, the pumps become generators and together have a 1-million-kilowatt generating capacity ◆

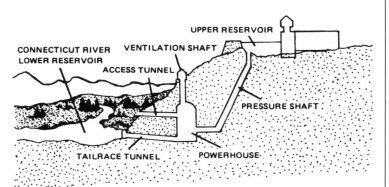

DIVERTING THE CONNECTICUT RIVER

Clean water is a valuable commodity. Even here in the well-watered Northeast it is not always found where it is needed. Eastern Massachusetts is the largest metropolitan area in New England and has had an increasing demand for water for 300 years. The construction of Quabbin Reservoir in 1936 was designed to meet this growing demand.

Now, 50 years later, still more water is being sought for the eastern part of the state. A series of alternatives are being studied by the state to increase the water supply for the Boston metropolitan area. Two of the alternatives would directly affect the Connecticut River. One would divert water from the Tully and Millers rivers, tributaries of the Connecticut River, to Quabbin Reservoir. The other would divert high flows from the Connecticut River itself through the Northfield Mountain System to Quabbin.

These proposals and others are very controversial. Many people are concerned about the environmental effects of reducing flows in these rivers. Changes in the freshwater content of the Connecticut River estuary and effects on migration of Atlantic salmon are some of the concerns being raised ◆

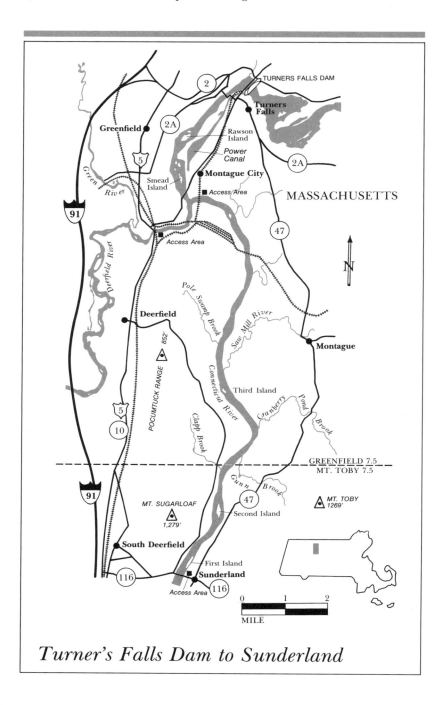

Turner's Falls Dam to Sunderland

Turner's Falls Dam to Sunderland

MILE:	117-106 (11 miles).
NAVIGABLE BY:	Kayak, canoe.
DIFFICULTY:	Flat water.
PORTAGES:	None.
CAMPING:	No established sites.
USGS:	Greenfield 7.5, Mt. Toby 7.5.

CAUTION: This section of the River is subject to sudden changes in the water level due to releases from Cabot Station in Turner's Falls. Do not camp or leave boats unsecured near the water's edge.

Starting at the Poplar Street portage area, veer left to follow the River's eastward flow. The Deerfield River [114.5] enters from the right directly across from the access area. A very pleasant side trip is to paddle up this river to the historic town of Deerfield, the site of the infamous Indian massacre of 1704. The town of Deerfield looks much the way it did 200 years ago, except that now it is a good deal more peaceful. Historic Deerfield, Inc. has 12 restored buildings that are open to the public and contain an outstanding collection of colonial furnishings. Call (413) 774-5581 for more information. Good launch sites on the Deerfield River are behind the tennis courts at Deerfield Academy, at the Rte. I-91 bridge, and at the Rte. 5 bridge.

Beginning at the Deerfield River, you may start to see schools of migratory fish such as shad that swim up the Connecticut River each year. South of the Deerfield River you will go under the first of two railroad bridges. Most of the fields are cultivated down to the riverbank. On this part of the River, you will occasionally catch views of the Pocumtuck Range to the west. Traveling under the second railroad bridge [112] you will reach Third Island, owned by the CRWC, at mile 110.5. The surrounding countryside is sparsely populated, with open cultivated fields and very quiet water. Just south of Clapp Brook on the west side is Whitmore's Ferry, where in low water the Jurassic age fish fossil beds can be seen.

If you are a geology buff, you will enjoy this stretch of the River. Mt. Toby is in the east, and North and South Sugarloaf Mountains in the west. The Sugarloaf Mountains get their names from their shape. These pedestal-like peaks are remnants of a type of igneous rock known as Sugarloaf Arkose that floors almost the entire valley. If you are beginning or ending your trip on the Connecticut River at the Rte. 116 bridge, you might want to take a short detour up Mt. Sugarloaf for a terrific view of the Connecticut River Valley.

The Rte. 116 bridge appears shortly after Mt. Sugarloaf, just south of First Island. There is a boat launch on the east side of the River. Groceries are available at a store located 1/4 mile east on School Street in Sunderland Center.

The River between Sunderland and Holyoke is home to New England's only endangered species of fish, the shortnose sturgeon.

THE BLOODY BROOK, TURNER'S FALLS AND DEERFIELD MASSACRES

In the fall of 1675 King Philip's War against the colonists reached the Connecticut River Valley when some of the local Indians allied themselves with King Philip, the sachem of the Wampanoags. The towns of Deerfield (Pocumtuck), Northfield (Squakeag), and Brookfield (Quaboag) were abandoned after Indian raids. The first attempt to evacuate Northfield met with disaster as Captain Beers and 36 men were ambushed and half of them killed just 2 miles before they reached the town on September 4. On September 18, 80 men under Captain Lathrop were ambushed on the way back from harvesting the crops at Deerfield. The spot near the foot of Mt. Sugarloaf was afterward called "Bloody Brook."

After a winter of starving on the run, many different groups of Indians gathered at the Peskeompscut (Turner's) Falls to fish, believing they were safe from attack. The commander of the garrison troops on the upper river towns, Captain Turner, heard of this and proceeded to the falls from Hatfield with 150 men on the night of May 18. He left his horse and crossed the river to one of the encampments, where his men shot into the wigwams of the sleeping Indians, killing 100 to 300 Indians, mostly women and children. Many fell or jumped to their deaths in the River or over the falls. Many Indians in nearby camps attacked the force in what became a panic-stricken rout back to Hatfield. One third of the men, including Turner, were killed.

The Deerfield Massacre itself occurred 29 years later in 1704, when marauding Iroquois Indians attacked on New Year's Eve, destroying the town and killing or capturing all but a few of the 270 inhabitants ◆

Frary House of 1740, Deerfield, MA.

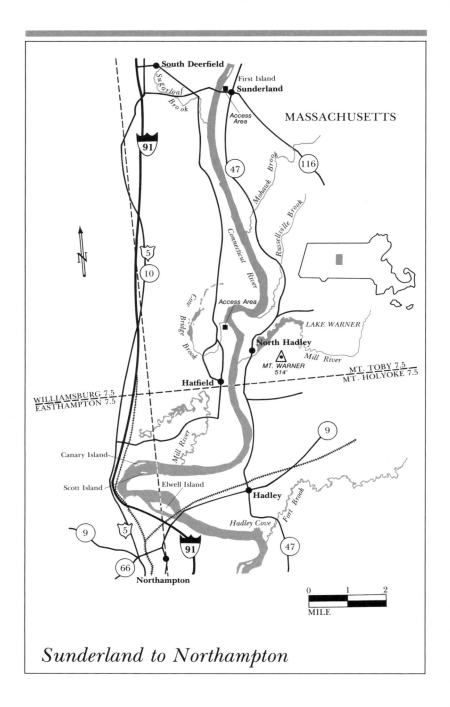

Sunderland to Northampton

Sunderland to Northampton

MILE:	106-92.5 (13.5 miles).
NAVIGABLE BY:	Kayak, canoe, small powerboats.
DIFFICULTY:	Flat water.
PORTAGES:	None.
CAMPING:	Mile 92.5; Sportsman's Marina; Hadley, MA; (413) 584-7141.
USGS:	Mt. Toby 7.5, Mt. Holyoke 7.5, Easthampton 7.5.

Sugarloaf Brook joins the Connecticut 1 mile after the Rte. 116 bridge. For the next several miles, high banks produce a tunnel-like atmosphere, although a wide cultivated floodplain of the Pioneer Valley extends on both sides. The Mohawk Brook [102.5] enters from the east as the River takes a 90-degree bend to the west. Cow Bridge Brook is a remnant brook flowing out of what is left of an earlier Connecticut River oxbow and harbors nesting ducks and heron. To reach the access area on Cow Bridge Brook by car, drive 1.5 miles north on Main Street from the center of Hatfield. Look for a dirt road (Kellogg Hill) that veers toward the River as the main road takes a sharp turn to the left.

Looking east, you can see Mt. Warner rising out of the floor of the former glacial Lake Hitchcock. The setting is very rural south of the Hatfield Oxbow. The banks are about 20 feet high, so it is hard to get a sense of the cultivated fields around you. For a long time, these fields produced some of the finest shade tobacco grown in the United States. The broadleaf tobacco was grown under muslin tents to protect the delicate leaves from the sun, and was used exclusively for the wrappers of cigars. Less costly means of production have been developed overseas, so that now there is very little tobacco grown in the valley. Strawberries, onions, corn, industrial parks, and shopping malls have replaced it.

The River remains straight for about 3 miles and then heads due west. The Mill River enters on the right or north side at mile 96. The Connecticut River takes a U-turn just after Canary Island [95]. You can paddle on either side of Elwell Island. Skipping across the tail end of Elwell Island is a railroad bridge, now converted to a bicycle path, and the Calvin Coolidge/ Rte. 9 Bridge [92.5] follows right on its heels at Northampton. On the left side is the Sportsman's Marina where boats can be launched or rented and camping is allowed with permission. A motel and restaurant are within an easy walk to the east on Rte. 9.

A few miles to the east of this section of the River is the town of Amherst, MA, where Amherst College (founded 1821), the University of Massachusetts (founded 1863), Hampshire College (chartered 1965), and the Emily Dickinson House are located. On the western bank of the River is the city of Northampton, the home of Smith College (founded 1875) and President Calvin Coolidge.

THE NEW HAVEN TO NORTHAMPTON CANAL

During the 1820's and 1830's, a fierce debate raged over how best to transport goods and people from the Connecticut coastline to central New England. Hartford and Middletown supported the improvement of the River with dredged channels, markers, and locks around the falls. New Haven businessmen, on the other hand, were jealous of all the trade traveling along the River.

Inspired by the success of the Erie Canal, they decided to build a canal from New Haven, CT, to Northampton, MA. In 1822 a company was chartered to build the 75-mile-long, 60-foot-wide canal with some 60 locks to overcome the 520-foot change in elevation. The first boat, drawn by five horses, went the length of the canal in 1835. For a dozen years, the canal and the River steamboats were rivals and competitors. However, the canal suffered from inadequate capitalization as well as from droughts and poor construction, and was finally closed in 1847 ◆

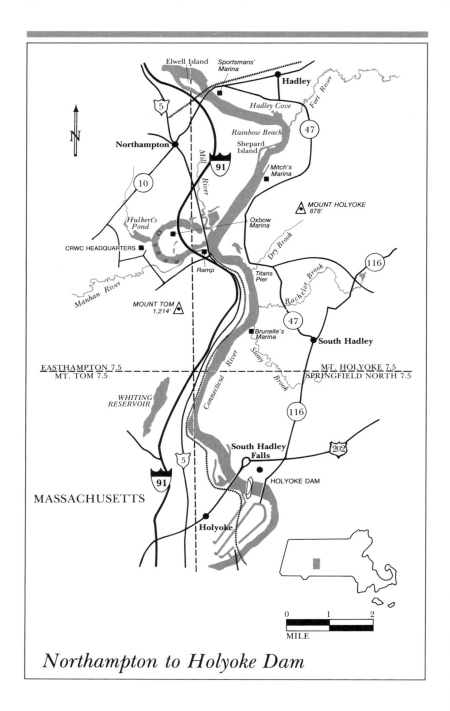

Northampton to Holyoke Dam

Northampton to Holyoke Dam

MILE:	92.5-81.5 (11 miles).
NAVIGABLE BY:	Kayak, canoe, small powerboats and sailboats.
DIFFICULTY:	Flat water.
PORTAGES:	Mile 81.5; Holyoke Dam; Vehicle-assisted portage: Mile 85.5; Brunelle's Marina; east side; 4 miles; see text and call HWP (413) 536-9441 during business hours, (413) 536-9458 or (413) 536-9449 at other times. Self-portage: Mile 81.5; east side; 1 mile.
CAMPING:	Mile 90; Rainbow Beach; Northampton, MA.
USGS:	Easthampton 7.5, Mt. Holyoke 7.5, Mt. Tom 7.5, Springfield North 7.5.

Leaving the Coolidge Bridge behind you, you will come to Hadley Cove, a favorite feeding ground for heron, egrets, sandpipers, and ducks. The Connecticut bends sharply to the right (south) at the confluence with the Fort River [90.5]. Good camping is available at Rainbow Beach on the west side of the bend. Less than a mile farther is Mitch's Marina on the left in Hadley. At the end of a 1½ mile-long straightaway, the former mouth of the Mill River enters above the junction of the Connecticut River and the Great Oxbow [88]. This remnant of the Mill River is not very good for paddling, since it serves as the outflow from the Northampton Wastewater Treatment Plant. The Mill River was diverted to flow through Hulbert's Pond and then into the oxbow.

If you go slightly farther south on the Connecticut River, you will reach the mouth of the Manhan River, which exits from the southern end of the oxbow. By passing under the railroad and highway bridges, you will enter the oxbow lake where a state boat ramp is located and is accessible from Rte. 5.

On the western side of the oxbow, you can explore Hulbert's Pond (which is also an ancient oxbow) and visit the headquarters of the Connecticut River Watershed Council and Massachusetts Audubon Society's Arcadia Wildlife Sanctuary. The sanctuary has several nature trails and exhibits, as well as a library. We also invite you to stop by the Watershed Council's headquarters for a cup of coffee or tales of the River. The Oxbow Marina is located around the oxbow on the north end and has a picnic area and launch. It is accessible from Rte. 5 off Island Road.

Directly to the east of the oxbow is the Mount Holyoke Range. Mt. Holyoke and Mt. Tom get their characteristic shape from the tough igneous rock of which they are made. The asymetrical slope of the mountains is due to an upward thrust along a fault line.

The Prospect House Hotel was built on the summit of Mt. Holyoke in 1851. Guests rode up to the summit on a horse-powered, cog railway in cars made from sleighs. Many artists and poets have ascended the peak to take in the magnificent 360-degree view of the valley and oxbow. If you are starting or stopping at this point, it is well worth taking a side trip up to the top of the mountain. You can either drive or hike up Mt. Holyoke from Rte. 47 in Hadley. A few miles away in South Hadley is Mt. Holyoke College, chartered in 1836.

The coal-fired Mt. Tom Power Plant, operated by Holyoke Water Power Company, is located a mile south of the oxbow. The 200-foot cliffs of Titan's Pier stand opposite the power plant on the east side. Bachelor Brook enters from the east at mile 86, and Stony Brook at mile 85.5.

Adjacent to Stony Brook is Brunelle's Marina, the start of the vehicle-assisted portage around the Holyoke Dam. The Holyoke Water Power Company provides a free canoe portage around the Holyoke Dam (4 miles downstream) from the marina. To avoid delays, call (413) 536-9441 during business hours (otherwise, 536-9458/9449) at least three days in advance of your planned arrival. Call again when you reach the marina. Other boaters and canoeists preferring a self-portage can proceed downstream.

The fossilized dinosaur tracks at Smith's Ferry are less than a mile south of the brook on the west side of the River. Watch for ledges jutting into the River right below where Rte. 5 rejoins the River. If you land at the access area at the foot of Old Ferry Road, you will find the dinosaur footprints in the shale outcropping between the highway and the railroad tracks.

CAUTION: At mile 84, the River narrows as it passes through a very deep gorge. Take care in this area because there can be rough water between the rock walls of the gorge.

The southern end of a peninsula [82] on the east bank is the start of the Holyoke Dam self-portage. If you choose to portage yourself, ascend the 10- to 20-foot bank to Canal Street in South Hadley. Walk along Canal Street until you are about 1/4 mile below the Rte. 116 bridge [81]. You can put in just beyond a playground under the bridge. There is a short unpaved ramp angling sharply off the road. It is not easy for trailers.

The Mueller Bridge (Rte. 202) spans the River just before the dam. Just above the bridge on the west bank is Log Pond Cove, a natural holding area for logging operations from the 1860's to the early 1900's. Logs were floated downriver to supply the paper mills of Holyoke. Murals of the cove can be seen in the Holyoke City Hall.

Although it is not accessible by boat, you may also want to plan a special trip to the Holyoke Dam to see the fish lift and exhibits. Since 1955, the elevators have lifted more than 4 million adult shad over the dam to continue their annual spawning migration. Call (413) 536-5520 for a visitor's permit. The ladder and elevators are especially active in May and June, and again during the fall salmon run.

Holyoke was the first planned industrial city in the United States. The entire city was mapped out to take advantage of the water power created by the falls and of the level land for factories and housing.

DINOSAURS

In 1802 a man by the name of Pliny Moody was plowing his field in South Hadley, MA, when he came across what looked like giant bird foot prints in a piece of brownstone. He was so intrigued that he made the stone into his front doorstep. Although he did not know it, Moody had found the first fossil evidence of dinosaurs in the New World. In 1818 the fossilized bones of a 6-foot-tall bird were unearthed in East Windsor, CT.

While the tracks and bones themselves were not very impressive, the existence of evidence of extinct species had profound implications. They meant that the Bible could not be interpreted literally because the rocks were too old, and in fact were made up of even older rocks from farther up the valley. Furthermore, Noah was supposed to have taken two of every species onboard the ark, leaving only the corrupt of humanity to perish in the floodwaters. Within a generation, the believed age of the earth went from roughly 6,000 years to 4.6 billion years.

Other dinosaur tracks were found in the soft sedimentary mud that later cemented into brownstone throughout the central valley of the Connecticut River. Perhaps the best, and certainly the best-preserved, dinosaur tracks were found in Rocky Hill, CT, by an alert bulldozer operator while constructing a state building in 1966. The 1,000 in situ tracks at Dinosaur State Park are protected by a 40-foot-high geodesic dome and have a boardwalk over them so that visitors can get a closeup look at the tracks made by the Dylophoarous, or "Double-armed Lizard," 185 million years ago. There is also a casting area where if you bring your own plaster, you can make casts of the prints. For more information on the park, call (203) 529-8423 ◆

CRWC Activities in Massachusetts

■ The Council continues to be a leader in opposing the diversion of the Connecticut River or its tributaries as a water supply for eastern Massachusetts.

■ The Council has protected wetlands, riverfront lands, islands, and forestlands through its land conservancy programs.

■ The Council is working to clean up pollution from combined sewer overflows along the River and its tributaries.

■ The Council conducts public canoe trips on the River and its tributaries.

EMILY DICKINSON

Emily Dickinson (1830-86) spent most of her life as a recluse in Amherst. During her lifetime, she published only seven poems. After her death, her sister found more than 1,000 other poems and arranged for their publication. A subsequent owner of the Dickinson house found more poems in an old box in the attic in 1915. Today Emily Dickinson is recognized as one of America's greatest poets. The Dickinson House is open to the public. Call (413) 542-2321 for more information ◆

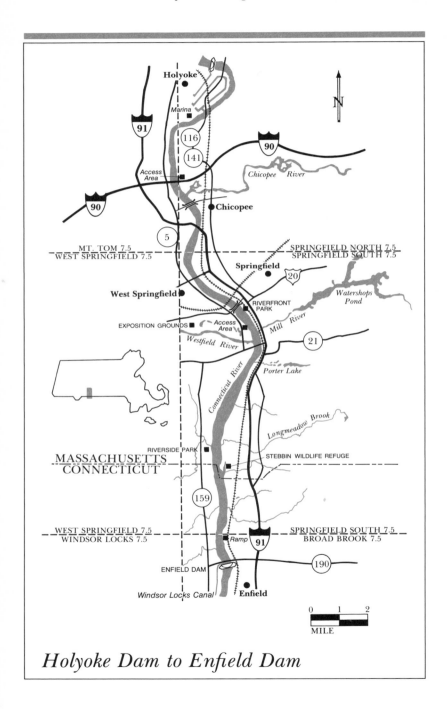

Holyoke Dam to Enfield Dam

Holyoke Dam to Enfield Dam

MILE:	81.5-63 (18.5 miles).
NAVIGABLE BY:	Kayak, canoe, small powerboats; also small sailboats between Springfield and Rte. 190 bridge.
DIFFICULTY:	Flat water.
PORTAGES:	Mile 63; Enfield Dam; west side; 300 yards.
CAMPING:	No established sites.
USGS:	Springfield North 7.5, Mt. Tom 7.5, Springfield South 7.5, Broad Brook 7.5.

At the put-in, ¼ mile south of the Rte. 116 bridge on Canal Street, the water can be low and may necessitate moving farther downstream. Continuing south, you will go under the Boston and Maine Railroad bridge and the adjacent Williamansett Bridge between Holyoke and Chicopee (Rte. 141), [79.5]. The area from Holyoke to Springfield is heavily populated, and the River is still polluted, primarily from combined storm and sanitary sewers that discharge untreated sewage into the River during heavy rainstorms. The River improves moderately as it passes through a residential area for about 4 miles.

There is a boat ramp under the Massachusetts Turnpike Bridge (Rte. I-90) [76] that can be reached off Granger Street and Rte. 116 in Chicopee on the east side. The improved but still badly polluted Chicopee River enters ½ mile south, further degrading the water quality of the Connecticut. Another access point is at the end of Hayes Road, close to Rte. 5. Shortly thereafter you will pass the site of the old West Springfield/Williamansett Bridge. At mile 74.5 you will pass below the Rte. I-91 bridge.

The River becomes more enjoyable as it enters and passes through Springfield. The beautiful granite North End Bridge will come into view at mile 72.5. Bassett's Marina is on the left bank just below the bridge. Then comes a Conrail bridge, followed by the Hampden County Memorial Bridge at mile 71.5. On the east bank just above the bridge is Northeast Utilities' oil- and coal-fired West Springfield Station generating plant. The Bondi's Island boat ramp is on the right, next to the sewage treatment plant and landfill. The large parking lot is easily reached from Rte. 5.

Springfield's waterfront area has recently been improved, affording a very nice view of the skyline with its 300-foot campanile. The new Basketball Hall of Fame adjoins Springfield's Riverfront Park.

A mile below this the Westfield River flows in from the west and the Mill River from the east. The Eastern States Exposition grounds are about a mile up the Westfield River on the right, just over the dike. On the left is Agawam Meadows where you can spot egrets and heron. On the south side of the Westfield is an access area at Pynchon Point Park off River Road.

The South End Bridge [70] immediately precedes the Springfield Yacht Club.

Beginning in Agawam you leave the urban setting and enter an agricultural area where the fields slope down to the River's edge. To the west, the roller coaster at Riverside Park is visible above the trees, and the screams from riders are often audible. There is good birding at Willy's Island near the Massachusetts/Connecticut border [66]. In the cutback just above Raspberry Brook on the east side is the Stebbin Wildlife Refuge, with several nature trails. Two miles below the border, by the old mill town of Thompsonville, you will come to the derelict piers of the old Rte. 190 bridge; the truss span was dismantled in 1971. There is a town boat ramp just south of the eastern abutment of this bridge.

Three-quarters of a mile farther is the new Rte. 190 bridge. At the western abutment is a Connecticut state boat ramp in Suffield, now closed to general use. This is where you must take out to portage the Enfield Dam, which is immediately downstream of the bridge.

■ *DANGER: Though the dam is now breached in several locations, running it is not recommended. The dam is 9 feet high and is skewed downstream to the west, where a canal lock once admitted boats into the Windsor Locks Canal.*

The waters below the dam are a popular shad-fishing area in the spring, although the dam's deterioration has reduced its ability to impede the shad's upstream migration and hence reduced the bottleneck that made the dam such a good fishing area.

From the boat ramp under the Rte. 190 bridge, the portage around the Enfield Dam is about ¼ mile to the canal just below the head lock. Alternatively, in the summer you can cross the upper gates of the head lock and return to the River from the towpath. See the Enfield Dam to Hartford section of this book for a complete description of the portage around the Enfield Dam.

THE ENFIELD RAPIDS AND THE WINDSOR LOCKS CANAL

Formerly known as Enfield Falls, the town of Windsor Locks stands just below the Enfield Dam at the head of tidewater navigation on the Connecticut River. The town owed its early importance to the River traffic and the neccessity of transferring cargo from tidewater vessels, carting it around the falls, and reloading it into flatboats for the remainder of the trip upstream. Only very small flatboats could be poled up the rapids. All other cargo had to be pulled overland in oxcarts. The portaging around the rapids continued for almost 200 years until 1829, when the canal and locks were built. The 5½-mile-long canal was an important link for 15 or more years, until the advent of the railroads effectively ended the use of steamboats on the upper River ◆

Shad fishing at the Enfield Dam.

A PLANNED INDUSTRIAL COMMUNITY

Holyoke has the distinction of being the first planned industrial community in the United States. It grew from a tranquil hamlet in the 1760's to the "paper city of the world" by the 1880's—with a population of 60,000.

In the 2 miles between Holyoke and South Hadley, the Connecticut River drops 60 feet. It was this natural feature of the River that, in 1846, attracted investors from the eastern part of the state. Recognizing the potential for water-power development, they organized as the Hadley Falls Company and acquired 1,100 acres of land on which they planned a new city, the foundations of which were a great dam and a system of canals.

An immense undertaking for its day, it attracted nationwide attention, and many manufacturing companies and waves of immigrant workers moved to the area. The plan provided areas not only for the mills but also for residents, stores, utilities, churches, a reservoir, parklands, and more. The 4-mile canal was laid out at three different elevations, permitting the water to be used several times over. The first dam had inherent design problems and collapsed on the day of its dedication but was rebuilt the following year in 1849.

A colorful account of the happenings on the day of the first dam's dedication was sent over the newly invented telegraph to the dam's investors in Boston:

10:00 A.M.   *Gates just closed; water filling behind dam.*

12:00 Noon   *Dam leaking badly.*

2:00 P.M.   *Stones of bulkhead giving way to pressure.*

3:20 P.M.   *Your old dam's gone to hell by way of Williamansett.*

The second Holyoke Dam lasted until 1900 when it was supplanted by the present 1,020-foot granite dam.

Textiles were Holyoke's earliest products, but were soon surpassed by paper. Holyoke continues today as one of the state's largest industrial cities, with a great diversity of products, textiles and paper included. For a truly interesting presentation of the story of Holyoke—complete with graphics and a guide/interpreter—a visit to Holyoke's Heritage Park is recommended ◆

Holyoke Dam.

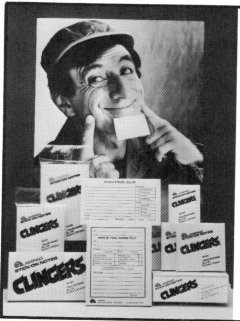

Connecticut

Marinas, docks and access points in Connecticut

Mile	Name	Parking	Ramp	Dock	Telephone	Water	Ice	Rest Rooms	Gasoline	Diesel Fuel	Transient Slips	Transient Moorings	Food / Hot ▼ Cold ●	Marine Supplies	Bait ▼ Tackle ●	Rent / Canoes ▼ Kayaks ●	Rent / Powerboats	Rent / Sailboats	Pump Out	Marine Railway ▼ Holst ●	Storage
65.5	Town Ramp, Enfield, CT South River St.	✓	✓																		
65	State Ramp, Suffield, CT off Canal Street	✓	✓																		
61	State Ramp, Enfield, CT off Parson's Street	✓	✓																		
57	Farmington River Ramp, Windsor, CT Pleasant St. off Rte. 159	✓	✓																		
55	Town Ramp, South Windsor, CT off Vibert Road	✓	✓																		
52.5	State Ramp, Windsor, CT below Bissell Bridge	✓	✓																		
49	Riverside Park, Hartford, CT off Rte. I-84, Exit 33	✓	✓																		
47.5	State Ramp, East Hartford, CT Pitkin Street off East River Dr.	✓	✓																		
45	Cove Park, Wethersfield, CT	✓	✓																		

Marinas, docks and access points in Connecticut

Mile	Name	Parking	Ramp	Dock	Telephone	Water	Ice	Rest Rooms	Gasoline	Diesel Fuel	Transient Slips	Transient Moorings	Food/Hot▼Cold●	Marine Supplies	Bait▼Tackle●	Rent/Canoes▼Kayaks●	Rent/Powerboats	Rent/Sailboats	Pump Out	Marine Railway▼Hoist●	Storage
37	Town Ramp, Glastonbury, CT off Tryon Street	✓	✓																		
37	Ferry Park, Rocky Hill, CT	✓	✓																		
30	Portland Riverside Marina, Portland, CT 37 Riverview St. (203) 342-1911	✓	✓	✓	✓	✓	✓	✓		✓	✓		✓						● ◄	✓	
29	Portland Boat Works, Portland, CT 1 Grove Street (203) 342-1085	✓	✓	✓	✓	✓	✓	✓		✓	✓		✓						●	✓	
29	Yankee Boat Yard & Marina, Portland, CT (203) 342-4735	✓	✓	✓	✓	✓	✓	✓		✓	✓		✓						● ◄	✓	
23	Hurd State Park, Haddam Neck, CT	✓		✓	✓																
20	Haddam Meadows State Park Haddam, CT	✓	✓				✓														
20	Connecticut Yankee Recreation Area Haddam Neck, CT	✓	✓	✓	✓	✓	✓	✓					✓								
17	Damar Ltd. Midway Marina, Haddam, CT (203) 345-8052	✓	✓	✓	✓	✓	✓	✓					✓						●	✓	

Deep River Navigation Company

Connecticut's
Largest Excursion
Boat Line

> *The Steam Train and Riverboat*
> *Saybrook Point Cruises*
> *Harborpark Cruises*

We offer a wide variety of daily riverboat cruises from Saybrook Point, Essex, Deep River and Middletown. Our modern well appointed riverboats are also available for private parties, weddings, business meetings and fund raising events on the Connecticut River and Long Island Sound.

Call or write for schedules and fares.

Deep River Navigation Company
River Street Box 312
Deep River, Connecticut 06417

(203) 526-4954

Marinas, docks and access points in Connecticut

Mile	Name	Parking	Ramp	Dock	Telephone	Water	Ice	Rest Rooms	Gasoline	Diesel Fuel	Transient Slips	Transient Moorings	Food / Hot ▼ Cold ●	Marine Supplies	Bait ▼ Tackle ●	Rent / Canoes ▼ Kayaks ●	Rent / Powerboats	Rent / Sailboats	Pump Out	Marine Railway ▼ Hoist ●	Storage
16.5	Salmon River State Ramp East Haddam, CT	✓	✓																		
15.5	Andrews Marina, Haddam, CT (203) 345-2286	✓	✓	✓	✓	✓	✓	✓	✓				✓		▲						
15.5	East Haddam Landings East Haddam, CT	✓	✓	✓																	
14	Town Landing, Chester, CT	✓	✓	✓							✓										
13	Chrisholm Marina, Chester, CT (203) 526-5147			✓	✓	✓	✓	✓	✓	✓	✓	▲●	✓						●	✓	
12.5	Gillette Castle State Park Hadlyme, CT	✓																			
11.5	Hay's Haven Marina, Chester, CT (203) 526-9366	✓		✓	✓	✓	✓	✓	✓	✓	✓	●	✓						●	✓	
9.5	Deep River Marina, Deep River, CT (203) 526-5360			✓	✓	✓	✓	✓	✓	✓	✓		✓						●	✓	
7.5	Old Lyme Marina, Old Lyme, CT (203) 434-1272	✓		✓	✓	✓	✓	✓	✓	✓	✓		✓						●	✓	

Marinas, docks and access points in Connecticut

Mile	Name	Parking	Ramp	Dock	Telephone	Water	Ice	Rest Rooms	Gasoline	Diesel Fuel	Transient Slips	Transient Moorings	Food / Hot ▼ Cold ●	Marine Supplies	Bait ● Tackle	Rent / Canoes ▼ Kayaks ●	Rent / Powerboats	Rent / Sailboats	Pump Out	Marine Railway ▼ Hoist ●	Storage
7.0	Cove Landing Marina, Old Lyme, CT (203) 434-5240	✓		✓	✓	✓		✓	✓	✓	✓	●	✓						◄●	✓	
6.0	Essex Island Marina, Essex, CT (203) 767-1267	✓		✓	✓	✓		✓	✓	✓	✓	◄●	✓						●	✓	
6.0	Town Ramp, Essex, CT Main Street		✓	✓																	
6.0	Connecticut River Foundation Main St., Essex, CT	✓	✓	✓																	
6.0	Essex Paint & Marine, Essex, CT (203) 767-8267	✓		✓	✓	✓	✓	✓		✓	✓		✓								
6.0	Essex Boat Works*, Essex, CT (203) 767-8276	✓		✓	✓	✓	✓	✓	✓	✓	✓		✓							✓	
6.0	Middle Cove Marina, Essex, CT (203) 767-1427	✓		✓	✓	✓	✓	✓											●		
3.5	Ragged Rock Marina, Old Saybrook, CT (203) 388-1049			✓	✓	✓		✓	✓	✓			✓						●	✓	
3.5	River Landing Marina†, Old Saybrook, CT (203) 388-1431	✓		✓	✓	✓		✓		✓		◄●	✓						●	✓	

*Full Service Yard
†Taxi Service

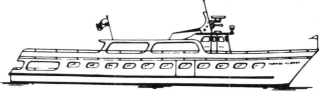

Marinas, docks, and access points in Connecticut

Mile	Name	Parking	Ramp	Dock	Telephone	Water	Ice	Rest Rooms	Gasoline	Diesel Fuel	Transient Slips	Transient Moorings	Food / Hot ▼ Cold ●	Marine Supplies	Bait ▼ Tackle ●	Rent / Canoes ▼ Kayaks ●	Rent / Powerboats	Rent / Sailboats	Pump Out	Marine Railway ▼ Hoist ●	Storage
3.5	Ferry Point Marina, Old Saybrook, CT (203) 388-3260	✓		✓	✓	✓	✓	✓	✓	✓			✓						▲	✓	
3.0	Oak Leaf Marina, Old Saybrook, CT (203) 388-9817	✓		✓	✓	✓	✓	✓	✓	✓			✓						▲	✓	
3.0	State Ramp, Old Saybrook, CT Under I-95 Bridge	✓	✓																		
2.5	Yacht Distributors Marina Old Saybrook, CT (203) 388-4466	✓		✓	✓	✓	✓	✓	✓	✓		▲●	✓	▲●			✓		●	✓	
2.5	Saybrook Point Marina, Old Saybrook, CT (203) 388-3862	✓		✓	✓	✓	✓	✓	✓	✓		▲●	✓								
1.0	Great Island State Ramp Old Lyme, CT, off Smith's Neck Rd.	✓	✓																		

Marinas, docks and access points in Connecticut

Mile	Name	Parking	Ramp	Dock	Telephone	Water	Ice	Rest Rooms	Gasoline	Diesel Fuel	Transient Slips	Transient Moorings	Food / Hot ▼ Cold ●	Marine Supplies	Bait ▼ Tackle ●	Rent / Canoes ▼ Kayaks ●	Rent / Powerboats	Rent / Sailboats	Pump Out	Marine Railway ▼ Hoist ●	Storage
W –*	Harry's Marine Repair, Westbrook, CT (203) 399-6165	✓	✓	✓	✓	✓	✓	✓	✓	✓			✓					✓	●		
W –	Pilot's Point Marina, Westbrook, CT (203) 399-7906	✓	✓	✓	✓	✓	✓	✓	✓	✓		▼●	✓	●					●	✓	✓
W –	Pier 76 Marina, Westbrook, CT (203) 399-7122	✓	✓	✓	✓	✓	✓	✓	✓	✓			✓						●	✓	✓
E –†	Rocky Neck State Park, Rocky Neck, CT (203) 739-5471	✓	✓																		

*W – West of Old Saybrook Lighthouse on Long Island Sound
†E – East of Old Saybrook Lighthouse on Long Island Sound

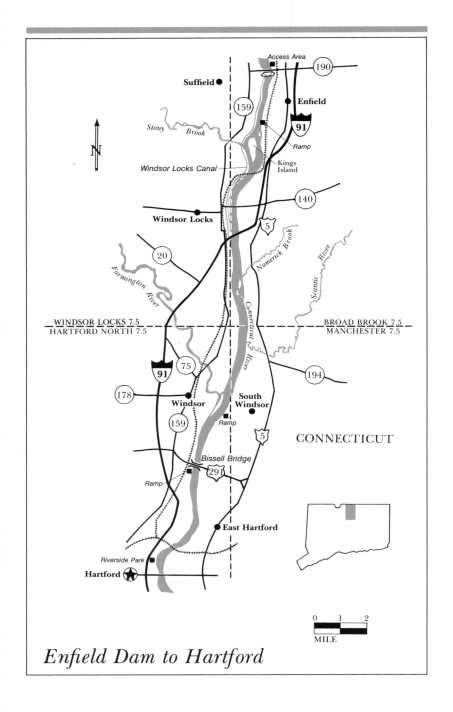

Enfield Dam to Hartford

Enfield Dam to Hartford

MILE:	63-49 (14 miles).
NAVIGABLE BY:	Kayaks, canoes, small powerboats, and sailboats near Hartford.
	Kayaks and canoes only on Windsor Locks Canal. Access restricted (see text).
DIFFICULTY:	Class I-II, flat water.
PORTAGES:	If the Windsor Locks Canal route is taken, there is a short portage to return to the River (see text).
CAMPING:	No established sites.
USGS:	Windsor Locks 7.5, Broad Brook 7.5, Manchester 7.5, Hartford North 7.5.

At the Enfield Dam you can choose to go downstream via the Windsor Locks Canal or the mainstream of the Connecticut River. Permission to paddle on the Windsor Locks Canal must be obtained in advance from the Windsor Locks Canal Company at (203) 623-9801. If you choose the canal, you will have an easy paddle for some 5 miles. At mile 60.5 the canal crosses Stony Brook in Suffield on a 100-foot aqueduct of antique design. When you reach the old center of Windsor Locks, the best opportunity to return to the River is at the north end of the first factory building you encounter on the canal bank. If you continue along the canal another mile to its end, ducking low to get under a few bridges, you will find three more antique locks. Unfortunately, a direct return to the River here is not feasible, but a ¼ mile portage along the adjacent highway will bring you to a suitable launching site under the Interstate 91 highway bridge.

At the time of this writing there are plans for the installation of a hydroelectric generating station on the canal. When and if this will happen and how it will affect boating on the canal are not known.

The alternative to the canal is to return to the River below the Enfield Dam. Novices are not encouraged to take the River. When there is sufficient water, the River can be quite enjoyable for experienced paddlers. This section of the River is very pretty, with high banks and cultivated fields to the east. You will pass the site of the first bridge across the Connecticut River in Connecticut a mile below the dam. The old covered bridge was carried away by ice in 1898. A boat-launching ramp is maintained by the State of Connecticut in Enfield at mile 61.

The River can be navigated on either side at Kings Island, but in low water the east channel is much better. Stony Brook enters into the west channel and is badly polluted from inadequately treated sewage. The canal aqueduct bridge across Stony Brook can be seen from the River.

The railroad bridge immediately following Kings Island is best passed, with care, under the long central truss span. This is the head of navigation from Long Island Sound, and also where you will begin to experience tidal fluctuations. A mile below the railroad bridge is the Rte. 140 highway bridge at Windsor Locks, followed in another mile by the Dexter Coffin Bridge (Rte. I-91). On the west bank just before this bridge are the three lower locks that link the Windsor Locks Canal with the Connecticut River.

The islands below Rte. I-91 [56] are sedimentary and shift over time. Stoughton Brook enters here from the east. The Scantic River enters within 2 miles, also from the east.

The entrance of the Farmington River is obscured by a large island at its mouth. This important tributary is a prime spawning ground for Atlantic salmon and American shad. The Farmington also offers some of the best whitewater sport in southern New England. If you have time, it is worth a trip up this river. A complete guide to the river can be obtained from the Farmington River Watershed Association, 749 Hopmeadow St., Simsbury, CT 06070, (203) 658-4442. You can put in or take out on the south bank under the Rte. 159 bridge on Pleasant Street. The Farmington will be difficult to paddle up if Rainbow Dam, 8½ miles upstream, is releasing water.

Just below the entrance of the Farmington, on the east bank of the River, is the South Windsor town ramp. The River will be getting steadily wider, so winds will be more and more of a concern to the small boater. The water is flat, but very shallow, with rocks and sandbars in many locations.

Under the Bissell Bridge, Rte. 291 [52.5] in Windsor, is a state boat ramp. There is another railroad bridge at mile 49.5. You can take out at Riverside Park in Hartford, where there is also a boat ramp. To get to the park by car, take Rte. I-91 and exit at the service roads (exit 33), the first road north of the Rte. 84 junction.

THE VALLEY'S FLOOD-CONTROL SYSTEM

Following the 1936 flood, Congress charged the U.S. Army Corps of Engineers to review the flood problem and propose a plan to minimize the potential for flood damage. The Flood Control Act of 1938 approved a flood-control plan consisting of 20 reservoirs and local protection projects (dikes, levees, and floodwalls) at seven major damage centers: Hartford, East Hartford, Springfield, West Springfield, Holyoke, Northampton, and Chicopee. The Flood Control Act of 1941 authorized the construction of large reservoirs in the upstream areas.

By 1970, 16 upstream reservoirs and seven local protection projects had been completed at a cost of $300 million. It is estimated that in a recurrence of the 1936 flood, over 90 percent of the damage would be avoided. Yet the system is not complete. To protect the damage centers from a "Standard Project Flood," the Corps recommended the construction of seven more upstream reservoirs. The "Standard Project Flood" is defined as the flood that can be expected from the worst combination of the various meteorological and hydrological conditions that are reasonably characteristic of the area. A Standard Project Flood would be the worst flood ever to hit the valley.

Today, if a Standard Project Flood were to occur, the dikes in all the above cities except Hartford would be overtopped. Hartford constructed its floodwalls to a height that would hold back the floodwaters even if the seven additional reservoirs were never built. The other six cities assumed that the reservoirs would be built and constructed their local protection works accordingly.

In 1976, *The River's Reach* was published by the New England River Basin Commission. It recommended that the seven additional reservoirs not be constructed, that the six cities raise their local protection, and that the valley's floodplains be managed to keep people away from flood-hazard areas. To date, the reservoirs have not been constructed, the dikes have not been raised, and the valley-wide floodplain management program recommended by *The River's Reach* has still not been instituted ◆

MARK TWAIN

Samuel Clemens, alias Mark Twain, first visited Hartford in 1868, writing,"Of all the beautiful towns it has been my fortune to see, this is the chief." Five years later, he moved with his wife to a rambling Victorian Gothic house he had built on Farmington Avenue. The first floor was decorated by Louis Comfort Tiffany; the kitchen was in the front of the house so the servants could see the goings-on in the street; and in the back was a room in the shape of a pilot's house. As *The Hartford Courant* noted, "The novelty displayed in the architecture of the building, the oddity of its internal arrangements, and the fame of its owner will all conspire to make it a house of note for a long time to come."

Twain wrote of his house, "To us, our house was not unsentient matter—it had a heart and soul. . . . It was of us, and we were in its confidence, and lived in its grace and the peace of its benediction. We never came home from an absence that its face did not light up and speak its eloquent welcome—and we could not enter it unmoved."

Adjacent to the Twain house is the home of Harriet Beecher Stowe, the author of *Uncle Tom's Cabin*. Both houses are now part of the Nook Farm complex and are open to the public. Call (203) 525-9317 for additional information ◆

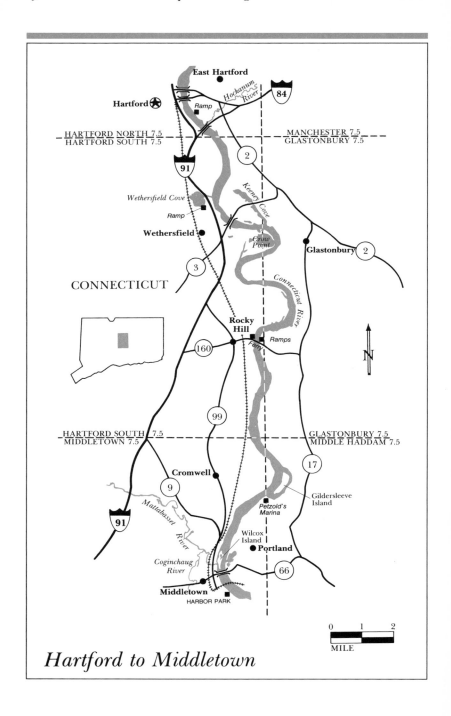

Hartford to Middletown

Hartford to Middletown

MILE:	49-30 (19 miles).
NAVIGABLE BY:	All craft with drafts less than 15' and mast heights less than 81' (below mile 47.5).
DIFFICULTY:	Flat water. (Beware of tides, winds, and boat wakes.)
PORTAGES:	None.
CAMPING:	No established sites.
USGS:	Hartford North 7.5, Hartford South 7.5, Glastonbury 7.5, Middletown 7.5, Middle Haddam 7.5.
NOAA:	Connecticut River: Bodkin Rock to Hartford (#12377).
RECOMMENDED:	Tidal Currents Tables; Atlantic Coast of North America (Dept. of Commerce), or Eldridge Tide Tables.

The best view of the Hartford skyline is from the Connecticut River just off Riverside Park. About ½ mile below the park you will pass under three highway bridges that lead directly into downtown Hartford. You will notice in the Morgan Bulkeley Bridge that the span closest to Hartford is made of metal, not stone, and is of a different design from the rest of the bridge. The bridge was built this way to facilitate the inclusion of a draw if it were later deemed necessary. There is a state boat ramp and dock in East Hartford between the Bulkeley and Founders bridges. The Park River enters the Connecticut River between the Founders and Charter Oak bridges at Hartford, but cannot be seen since it was covered over by the city because of heavy pollution and frequent flooding. Combined sewer overflows from Hartford may contaminate an 8- to 16-mile stretch of the River south of Hartford for several days after a heavy rainfall.

The Charter Oak Bridge will be reached at mile 47.5. Hartford was the home of Mark Twain and Harriet Beecher Stowe, among others, and has much to offer any visitor, although there is not a very good spot available to leave your boat while on a side trip. At the time of this writing, however, a docking area is under construction.

CAUTION: From below the Charter Oak Bridge the Army Corps of Engineers dredges a channel at least 15 feet deep and 150 feet wide. Coastal tankers and oil barges come as far north as Hartford. No other freight is regularly shipped on the Connecticut River. All boats must yield the right of way to the large and not very easily maneuvered oil barges. Small craft will want to keep an eye out for the wakes these boats can produce. However, a greater danger for small boaters is the wakes that large pleasure craft kick up. These wakes are large enough to capsize even skillful canoeists. Large-boat operators, please remember to slow down when near a canoe or other small boat. It is both a common courtesy and the law. Small-boat operators, please remember to stay out of the main channel to allow larger boats room to maneuver.

The entrance to Wethersfield Cove is on the west at mile 45. The very narrow inlet is marked with privately maintained navigational aids. Less than 200 years ago, the mainstream of the Connecticut River flowed past the warehouse in what is now the cove, until the current cut itself short and created an oxbow. The cove was further separated from the River by the construction of Rte. I-91. The bridge over the entrance to the cove limits the height of boats that can enter the cove to those under 30 feet. The colonial town of Wethersfield has a historical district with many fine houses that are open to the public and are worth visiting. There is a public ramp and dock in the cove.

After the cove you will pass under the Putnam Bridge (Rte. 3) between Wethersfield and Glastonbury. Crow Point and the Crow Point basin follow on the west as the River bends south. The basin was created by dredging for fill to be used in the construction of Rte. I-91. The basin has an average depth of about 4 feet and a good bottom if you want to drop anchor.

The next several miles offer attractive scenery and plenty of sandy beaches on which to picnic. Hall's Landing Marina is located on the right bank just above the town of Rocky Hill [37.5]. The oldest ferry in continuous operation in the country runs across the Connecticut River between Rocky Hill and Glastonbury. It holds about six cars, and has no fixed schedule. You may call the ferry by honking your horn. Do not use the ferry slip as a landing site. There are town ramps near the ferry landing on both sides of the River.

Dinosaur State Park is located a few miles from the River in Rocky Hill. If you bring your own plaster, you can make castings of some of the tracks. Call (203) 529-8423 for information.

For the next 8 miles the River is fairly straight and passes through hilly, wooded countryside. Gildersleeve Island will appear at mile 33.5. Small boats may find the shallower western side of the island a pleasant escape from the traffic in the main channel on the east side of the island.

CAUTION: There is a submerged dike across the northern end of the western side of Gildersleeve Island. The dike was built to direct the water to the east side of the island in order to keep the main channel open.

There is a landing site opposite Gildersleeve Island to the east off Rte. 17A in Portland. On the west side of the River is Riverside Marine Park with a concrete ramp, restaurant, and picnic tables. By this time small boaters will want to keep an eye on the tides and use them to advantage. Tide schedules can be found in local papers or at marinas.

Medium to large boats should keep to the east side of Wilcox Island [29.5], although shallow-draft boats may again find the other side less congested, hence more pleasant. A good selection of bird-life can be found in the extensive marshes up the Mattabasset River just north of Middletown. The Arrigoni Bridge, Rte. 66 [30.5], spans the River from Middletown to Portland. Just below it stands the railroad bridge that was partially destroyed in 1876 when the pilot of the steamship *The City of Hartford* confused the bridge lights with lights on shore and rammed the bridge. As a result of the accident, a national standard was set that all bridges must have red and green lights; not the white lights that had been used previously.

Another half mile will bring you to Middletown's Harbor Park, which has a public dock, a restaurant, and picnic tables. Wesleyan University's boat house is also at the park, and the Head of the Connecticut Regatta, one of the largest rowing races in the East, is held here every fall. The City of Middletown is one block away, and you will be able to find anything you need within a three-block walk of the River. Regularly scheduled cruises on the River are available from Middletown during the summer, as well as special fall foliage trips. The town of Portland is also within an easy walk from the River, to the east. There are no public docks, but you can tie up at one of the marinas for a small fee.

RIVERFRONT REVITALIZATION EFFORTS

In the mid-1800's, riverfront communities began to turn their backs on the Connecticut River. The River was being used as a sewer to carry away wastes from industrialization and a growing population. The construction of rail lines, later dikes, and an interstate highway completed the separation of the valley's major cities from what had been the wellspring of their prosperity.

The cities of Middletown, CT, and Springfield, MA, have led the way in reviving their waterfronts. By the late 1970's, $1.7 million in public funds had been allocated to the revitalization of Middletown's Harbor Park. Today, there is a picnic area, public dock, restaurant, and a boathouse for school rowing teams. Harbor Park serves as a staging area for concerts, festivals, river cruises, and rowing events such as the Head of the Connecticut Regatta, the second-largest in the East. The city is currently examining potential uses of the riverfront land south of Harbor Park.

In Springfield, MA, a riverfront commission spearheaded the effort to create a riverfront park. The park was upgraded in the 1970's through a community River design project. The park hosts a summer concert series and a rowing regatta. In 1985 a docking facility was installed. A short walk from the park and sharing riverfront space is the new Basketball Hall of Fame. A comprehensive development plan for Springfield's riverfront is underway.

The most ambitious and challenging effort underway is Riverfront Recapture in Hartford and East Hartford. More than any other city in the valley, Hartford has had its access to the River effectively cut off by the construction of a dike and highway. Riverfront Recapture, Inc. (RRI) is the nonprofit organization

Hartford Skyline.

formed in 1981 that is leading the revitalization effort. The master plan includes the development of parks, a 6-mile walkway from Windsor to Wethersfield, docking facilities, and some commercial development. A major obstacle was overcome when the State Department of Transportation agreed to redesign Interstate 91 when rebuilding the highway, thus allowing access to the River from downtown Hartford. RRI sponsors and cosponsors numerous events, including the July 4th River Festival on the Connecticut River ◆

THE OLD STATE HOUSE

Nestled among the modern skyscrapers in downtown Hartford is the Old State House, built in 1793 and designed by the famous architect Charles Bulfinch. Now fully restored to its original beauty, the Old State House was threatened with demolition on several occasions. A wide range of public events are now held at the Old State House and the adjoining park.

The Bulfinch State House replaced an earlier wooden structure that was severely damaged by an accidental fire that broke out during a fireworks demonstration celebrating the news of the peace treaty with Great Britain that recognized American independence. Abraham Davenport immortalized himself in this earlier state house on May 19, 1780, during an eclipse of the sun. When the sky became so dark that some feared that the Judgment Day was about to come, Davenport said to his colleagues: "I am against adjournment. The Day of Judgment is either approaching or it is not. If it is not, there is no cause for adjournment; if it is, I choose to be found doing my duty. I move therefore that candles be brought" ◆

The Connecticut River,
New England's Historic Waterway
by Edmund Delaney

The panoramic story of life along New England's 410-mile river, from colonial times to the present, from the Canadian border to Long Island Sound. A detailed appendix features a town-by-town guide to the major historic sites and museums along the river. 100 illustrations and photographs. Maps. Bibliography. Index. Appendix. 182 pages paperbound. The Globe Pequot Press.

"Using intensive research, sprinkled with a style that illustrates his dry wit and succinct way of getting to the heart of a subject, Delaney has written a history book that is fun to read." — The Hartford Courant

"We all have needed for a long time a really good book on the river, and this volume fills that need remarkably well." — Albert Van Dusen, Connecticut State Historian

"The Connecticut and the Mississippi have in common the fact that so much of our nation's history was written along their banks. . . . What a wealth of material! A splendid book." — J. Raymond Samuel, author of Tales of the Mississippi

$9.95 plus $1.00 postage. Conn. residents add .75 tax.

ORDER THROUGH CONNECTICUT RIVER WATERSHED COUNCIL PUBLICATIONS, Box 359, Chester, CT 06412

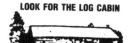

Rocky Hill/Glastonbury Ferry.

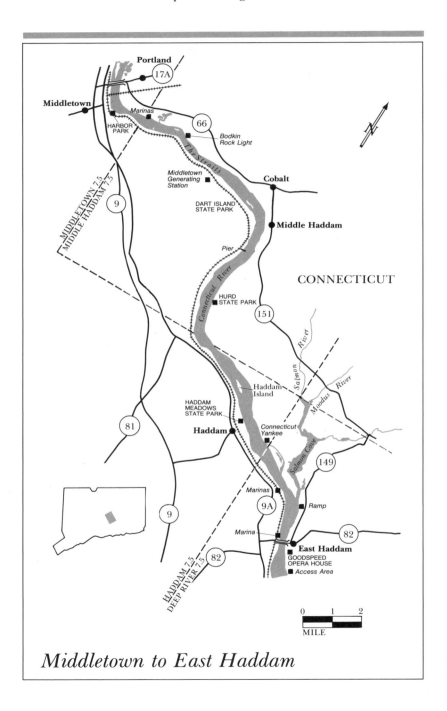

Middletown to East Haddam

Middletown to East Haddam

MILE:	30.5-15.0 (15.5 miles).
NAVIGABLE BY:	All craft with drafts less than 15' and mast heights less than 81'.
DIFFICULTY:	Flat water. (Beware of tides, wind, and boat wakes.)
PORTAGES:	None.
CAMPING:	Mile 25.5; Dart Island State Park; CT Dept. of Parks and Recreation; (203) 566-2304. Mile 23.0; Hurd State Park; Haddam Neck, CT; (203) 526-2336.
USGS:	Middletown 7.5, Middle Haddam 7.5, Haddam 7.5, Deep River 7.5.
NOAA:	Connecticut River: Bodkin Rock to Hartford (#12377), Deep River to Bodkin Rock (#12377).
RECOMMENDED:	Tidal Currents Tables: Atlantic Coast of North America (Dept. of Commerce) or Eldridge Tide Tables.

Car-topped boats can be put in at Harbor Park in Middletown. Trailered boats will have to go across the bridge to one of the marinas in Portland to be put in.

Below Middletown the River changes in character. No longer a shallow channel meandering through a wide floodplain, it now flows through a geologically older area of hills composed of metamorphic rock, shists, gneiss, and pegmatite. The River is generally wider, deeper, and straighter. The banks are high and ledgy, and are covered by mixed forests of oak, hemlock, and many other species.

Leaving downtown Middletown and Portland (site of the quarries that supplied stone for New York City's famous brownstone buildings), you will pass the WCNX broadcast tower on the right bank. Just below it is one of the concrete towers that house the Telemark advance flood warning system.

In a few hundred yards you will pass Bodkin Rock Light and enter the Straits. Here you can see excellent examples of the greatly folded metamorphic rock. Cut into the right bank is a feldspar mine and processing plant. Another mile brings you to the oil-fired

Middletown Station operated by Northeast Utilities on the west bank.

At mile 25.5 lies Dart Island State Park, which is an island only during high water. Across the River on the east side, a sandy beach provides a landing for the beautiful old town of Middle Haddam. Nearby, the Cobalt Mine has been worked intermittently since 1762 for cobalt, mica, nickel, and other minerals. A short distance from the River is a 40-foot waterfall on Mine Brook.

Throughout colonial times and well into the 19th century, a shipbuilding industry flourished in the small towns along the River like Middle Haddam. More than 4,000 ships were built, including early transatlantic packet ships. The local oak and hemlock trees, as well as wood floated down from upstream, provided the lumber these shipyards required.

At mile 24.5 a sewage-treatment plant pier juts out from the west bank. Following it is Pratt and Whitney Aircraft's pier, also jutting out from the west bank.

Hurd State Park [23], on the east side, offers good swimming, hiking, and camping. It can be recognized by the long breakwater that runs for most of its length. From here all the way to the Sound the water in the Connecticut River is Class B: suitable for fishing, and swimming.

Just south of Hurd State Park are the high-tension power lines from the Connecticut Yankee Atomic Power Company. At mile 20 is Haddam Island State Park. Its excellent sand beach is a good spot for picnicing and swimming, but camping is not allowed.

Operated by Northeast Utilities, the power plant [20] is one of the oldest commercial nuclear facilities in the country. It has set a world record of 417 days of uninterrupted operation. The plant also holds the U.S. record for the most power generated by a single nuclear unit. Boaters are welcome to tie up at the plant's dock and visit the Energy Information Center. There is also an adjacent picnic area with tables and hibachis. For further information, call (203) 267-9279.

Directly opposite Connecticut Yankee is Haddam Meadows State Park, which has two ramps, a picnic area, and softball fields. The meadows are the terminus of the Connecticut River Raft race held each summer, in which dozens of homemade rafts compete in various classes.

By keeping to the eastern shore after Haddam Meadows, you will pass the cooling-water discharge canal from the power plant. The canal is closed to boats, but fishermen are welcome to wet a line for the fish that are attracted to the warm water.

Mile 16.5 is the entrance to Salmon Cove and the Salmon River. There is a large, state-maintained ramp at the entrance to the cove. The marshes and backwaters of the river and cove offer excellent birding opportunities. Shallow-draft boats can go approximately 4 miles upstream to the fish ladder at the Leesville Dam on the Salmon River.

CAUTION: The channel through Salmon Cove is very narrow and windy. Pay strict attention to the tides, since most of the cove is only a foot deep at low tide. The upper Salmon River is a great spot for fishing and spring and fall whitewater boating.

A mile downstream of the Salmon River is the East Haddam Rte. 82, Bridge [15.5]. It is one of the oldest and largest swivel, or turnstile, bridges in the country. East Haddam is the home of the famous Goodspeed Opera House and the Nathan Hale School House. What is purported to be the oldest bell in the country (cast A.D. 815), hangs in Saint Stephen's Episcopal Church in East Haddam. It is a beautiful town with much to offer. Take some time to explore it.

You can tie up at either Goodspeed's Landing or at the town dock just below it. For longer stays, you can tie up at Andrews Marina across the River in Haddam. There is an unimproved dirt ramp just south of the Goodspeed Opera House's parking lot where you can take out. The ramp at Goodspeed Airport is for the seaplanes and should not be used without permission.

See the East Haddam to Essex chapter of this book for information about the East Haddam Bridge.

THE GOODSPEED OPERA HOUSE

Built in 1876, the Goodspeed Opera House is a fine example of the Victorian style. Lavishly decorated, a touch eccentric, it not only held a 400-seat theater, a bar, and offices but also a post office, a dry-goods store, and a freight warehouse. Its builder, William Goodspeed, had things well planned for the passengers on his steamship line traveling to Hartford or New York. While the boat was being loaded and unloaded, passengers could watch a Broadway play at his theater. Then they could have a meal on-board ship or at the restaurant conveniently located next door to the theater.

Falling into disrepair, the opera house was threatened by the wrecking ball in 1963. At the eleventh hour, the building was sold by the state to a nonprofit organization for one dollar. After extensive reconstruction, the opera house is today the nation's premier theater devoted to the American musical comedy. The Broadway hits *Man of La Mancha, Annie,* and *Shenandoah* were first performed here. Tours of the theater are available by calling the box office at (203) 873-8668 ◆

Connecticut River Real Estate

ROOT AGENCY
28 Main Street
East Haddam CT
(203) 873-8619

Equal Housing Opportunity 🏠
INDEPENDENTLY OWNED
AND OPERATED

OFFICE
Open 7 days

JOHNSON
OUTBOARDS

Hilltop Marine & Auto Inc.
ROUTES 16 & 149   COLCHESTER, CT.
267-2158

JOHN HOBAN
President

STARCRAFT
BOATS

TUOHY REALTY
Saybrook Road
Higganum, Connecticut 06441
Business 345-8116

ALBERTA S. TUOHY, CRB
Broker

CRWC Activities in Connecticut

■ The Council has protected more than 1,200 acres of land, including the 700-acre Spalding Pond Reserve in Norfolk, CT.

■ The Council co-founded the Connecticut Clean Water Coalition.

■ The Council is working to ensure long-term funding for municipal sewage projects.

■ The Council sponsors River-oriented special events and an educational canoe program for the public and inner-city youth.

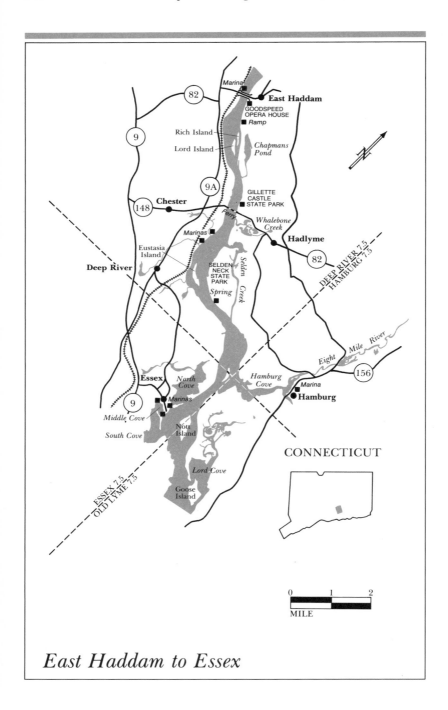

East Haddam

Marina

82

GOODSPEED
OPERA HOUSE
Ramp

9

Rich Island
Lord Island

Chapmans
Pond

9A

GILLETTE
CASTLE
STATE PARK

148   Chester

Ferry

Whalebone
Creek

Marinas

Hadlyme

82

DEEP RIVER 7.5
HAMBURG 7.5

Eustasia
Island

Deep River

SELDEN
NECK
STATE
PARK

Spring

Selden Creek

Eight Mile River

156

Essex

North
Cove

Hamburg
Cove

Marina

Hamburg

9

Marinas

Middle Cove

South Cove

Nott
Island

CONNECTICUT

Lord Cove

ESSEX 7.5
OLD LYME 7.5

Goose
Island

0   1   2

MILE

East Haddam to Essex

East Haddam to Essex

MILE:	15.5-6.0 (9.5 miles).
NAVIGABLE BY:	All craft with drafts less than 15′ and mast heights less than 81′.
DIFFICULTY:	Flat water. (Beware of tides, winds, and boat wakes.)
PORTAGES:	None.
CAMPING:	Mile 12.5; Gillette Castle State Park; Hadlyme, CT; (203) 526-2336.
	Mile 11.5; Selden Neck State Park; Hadlyme, CT; (203) 526-2336.
USGS:	Deep River 7.5, Hamburg 7.5, Essex 7.5, Old Lyme 7.5.
NOAA:	Connecticut River: Deep River to Bodkin Rock (#12377), Long Island Sound to Deep River (#12375).
RECOMMENDED:	Tidal Currents Tables; Atlantic Coast of North America (Dept. of Commerce) or Eldridge Tide Tables.

When closed, the East Haddam bridge has a vertical clearance of 24 feet at mean low water. If this will not allow you to pass, you can blow your horn three times, or call the bridge keeper on VHF channel 13 on your radio. There is considerable road traffic across the bridge. Opening the bridge can cause a traffic jam in East Haddam, so the bridge keeper may wait until there are several boats before opening.

From the East Haddam bridge to the Sound the banks of the River are subject to development restrictions overseen by the Connecticut River Gateway Commission, which was formed to preserve the scenic qualities of the lower valley.

Below East Haddam the River begins to widen out as the tidal effects become more and more pronounced. Staying to the east after the bridge, you will come to Rich and Lord islands. At the downstream end of Rich Island [14] is the entrance to Chapman's Pond, which is owned by the Nature Conservancy. The pond is ecologically unique because it is both tidal and freshwater. It is very pretty and a good place to look for osprey and heron. There is also very good fishing in the pond. Canoeists and shallow-draft fishing boats (proceed at no-wake speed) will find the pond and creek a pleasant side channel away from the noise of the main channel. You can continue south via Chapman's Creek, which exits at the southern end of the pond through a marshy area.

On the main River the Middletown Yacht Club is directly across from the south end of Lord's Island on the west bank.

Another mile will bring you to Gillette Castle State Park. You can't miss it: It looks like a melting castle sitting high on top of a hill overlooking the River. The castle is open to the public and makes a fascinating side trip, especially if the weather is good, because the view is spectacular. Call (203) 526-2336 for more information. You can camp or just beach and swim at the park, which is just north of the Chester/Hadlyme Ferry slip [12.5].

The Chester/Hadlyme Ferry has been in continuous operation since 1768. The ferry has no fixed schedule, and is called by a honk of a car horn. North of the ferry slip on the west bank is Chrisholm Marina, where food and some supplies can be found.

CAUTION: Because the main channel runs in close to the east bank, boaters should anchor on the west side of the River above the ferry.

One hundred yards south of the ferry is a navigational light at the entrance to Whalebone Creek. On one side of the creek is a big sandbar, and on the other side is an enormous rock wall. Small boats will find this a good place to disappear and do some birding in the marshes just upstream.

At mile 11.5 are the entrances to Selden Creek in the east and Chester Creek on the opposite side of the River in the west. Chester Creek has two marinas and the Pattaconk Yacht Club at its mouth and can be canoed almost all the way into the center of town. Chester has recently gone through a renaissance, and has many fine shops and restaurants. It is the home of the National Theater of the Deaf and the Norma Terris Theater.

To the east, Selden Cove is at the northern end of Selden Island, which happens to be the largest island in the state of Connecticut. The island is a state park with several campsites. The cove itself is very shallow; the channel is close to the island. Medium-draft powerboats and sailboats can safely navigate the cove and creek at a slow pace. The small boats will invariably find the cove and creek more relaxing than the wide-open and busy main channel. There is a lovely anchorage for deep-draft boats about one third of the way up the creek from the southern end of the island at the base of a high rock wall.

If you choose to stay in the main channel, it is well worth a stop at the freshwater spring on Selden Island, about a third of a mile south of the F1 R "36." Here, in the 17th and 18th centuries, many vessels—especially those in the African ivory trade, stopped to fill their water butts. Be sure to bring an empty jug.

Due west of the spring on Selden Island is Eustasia Island. Eustasia Island can be navigated on either side by medium-draft boats, although you should keep a close eye on the charts. Behind the island is Deep River Landing or Steamboat Landing, where the Valley Railroad steam train meets with a cruise boat for regularly scheduled sight-seeing trips on the River.

To sail south in the old steamboat channel to the east of Eustasia Island, head in toward Chester Creek, then follow the River back south about 50 to 100 feet offshore. Leave the concrete base of the old lighthouse that used to mark this channel to port (left). Opposite this is the mouth of the Deep River stream. After passing Deep River Marina, run pretty much in the middle but favor the starboard (right) or west side of the River until you pass F1 G "35" to port and are once again in the main channel.

The imposing building up on the bluff in Deep River is Mt. Saint John's School, which offers special care for troubled boys.

Another good side trip is into Hamburg Cove, one of the finest harbors in the state, and up the Eight Mile River. The channel into the cove looks uninspiring, with a sandbar on one side and rotting stumps on the other. The narrow passage is well marked, but a slow and cautious approach is recommended. At the height of the season the cove can be full of boats and a little hot, since not much wind gets into it. Regardless of the weather, the cove is beautiful and makes a superb anchorage, especially if a gale or hurricane is predicted.

South and west of Hamburg Cove is Great Meadow and the North Cove of Essex. Many migratory birds stop at this wide-open marsh area. Deep-draft boats should not go into the cove. Better deep-water anchorages are available in the other coves of Essex. Essex is a very attractive and historic old town with many beautiful houses, interesting shops, and excellent restaurants. There is a town dock and ramp at the foot of Main Street, and everything you could ever want for your boat is available from one of the chandleries in town.

The Connecticut River Foundation (CRF) at Steamboat Dock is right next door to the town dock. The CRF museum has many interesting exhibits, including a working model of the first submarine, designed by David Bushnell of Westbrook. For more information, call (203) 767-8269.

GILLETTE CASTLE

What looks like an old castle sitting high on a hill overlooking the Connecticut River was once the home of the actor William Gillette and is now Gillette Castle State Park. A native son of Connecticut, Gillette traveled to New York where he immortalized himself portraying Sherlock Holmes. Taking time off from the stage, Gillette took a leisurely cruise up the Connecticut River in 1913. He found the area so enchanting that he gave up his plans to build a house on Long Island and instead bought 122 acres in Hadlyme, CT. After five years and a million dollars, Gillette had finished his castle atop a hill known as "The Seventh Sister."

Every detail inside the castle and out was of Gillette's own design: the 4-foot-thick stone walls, the hand-carved oak doors, the light switches, even the serpentine driveway from the ferry landing. However, Gillette's pride and joy was his private railroad—two steam engines and three miles of narrow-gauge track that ran throughout the property over ornate bridges, through a tunnel, and along the edge of the River. Gillette's other hobbies included caring for 15 cats, several goldfish, and two pet frogs that he kept in the pool in the conservatory.

Chester/Hadlyme Ferry and Gillette Castle.

Before he died in 1937, Gillette directed his executors "to see that the property did not fall into the hands of some blithering saphead who has no conception of where he is or with what surrounded." Faithful to his wishes, his executors saw that the Castle became a state park in 1943. The trains and track have since been dismantled, but many of the elegant bridges are still part of the park's trails. Exploring the castle and the grounds is a great way to spend a few hours, especially if the weather is good, since the view of the Connecticut River is terrific. Call the park manager for more information at (203) 526-2336 ◆

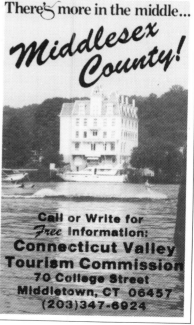

SELDEN ISLAND

Selden Neck State Park is actually the largest island in the state of Connecticut. It is also an excellent camping area and has several peaceful and beautiful deep-water anchorages. The island, however, was not always so quiet. During the American Revolution, Essex shipowners used to hide their boats along the creek and in the cove to keep them safe from British raids.

In the latter part of the 19th century there was a great demand for building stone and paving blocks for New York City and Philadelphia. Selden's Neck, Joshua's Rock, and Brockway's Landing were all sites of large quarries. More than 600 stonecutters, most from Italy, were housed and fed in barracks built for the purpose at the quarries. The stones were cut to the required sizes on the spot and then shipped directly downriver. By the end of the century, however, cement had become a more economical alternative, and the quarrying industry came to an end. Remnants of the quarry machines can still be found near the southern end of the island on the River side.

During Prohibition several stills reportedly operated in the marshes on the creek side, and the island was also a hideaway for rum-running smugglers' boats.

If you want to camp on Selden Island, call the park manager at (203) 526-2336 ◆

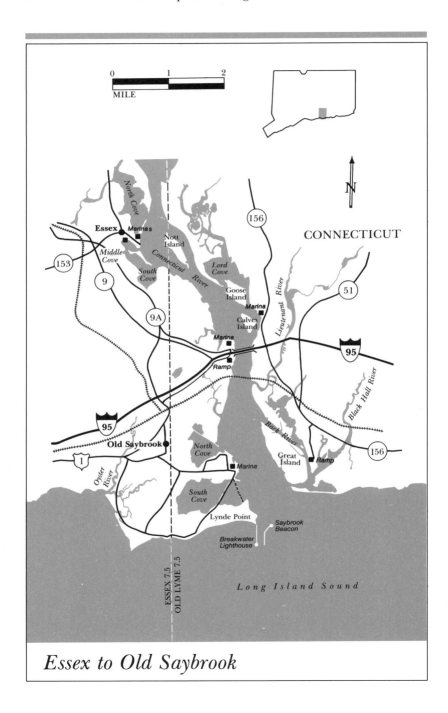

Essex to Old Saybrook

Essex to Old Saybrook Lighthouse

MILE:	6.0-0.0 (6 miles).
NAVIGABLE BY:	All craft with drafts less than 15' and mast heights less than 81'.
DIFFICULTY:	Flat water. (Beware of tides, winds, and boat wakes.)
PORTAGES:	None.
CAMPING:	No established sites.
USGS:	Essex 7.5, Old Lyme 7.5.
NOAA:	Connecticut River: Long Island Sound to Deep River (#12375).
RECOMMENDED:	Tidal Currents Tables; Atlantic Coast of North America (Dept. of Commerce) or Eldridge Tide Tables.

The town of Essex maintains a ramp and dock at the foot of Main Street. Car-topped and trailered boats can be put in here, although there isn't very good parking for trailers. The first American warship, the *Oliver Cromwell*, was built on this spot in 1775. British marines raided Essex in 1814 and destroyed some 23 ships at anchor or under construction. No lives were lost, but several barrels of rum were reported missing.

Those in small boats might enjoy exploring the coves around Essex. Larger boats can anchor in Middle Cove and can go a short way into North Cove, but should not try to enter South Cove. A current navigational chart is essential if you want to explore these coves in anything more than a canoe or dinghy. Middle Cove makes a very nice, quiet, and well-protected anchorage with a good holding bottom. The channel into the cove has a reported depth of 6 feet. Another good "gunk hole," where you can anchor away from the crowds, is on the far side of Nott Island, across the River from Essex. This anchorage can be approached only from the south, due to shallow water on the north side of the island. All of the coves and Nott Island are excellent areas for birding because of the extensive marshes that surround them.

About 2 miles south-southeast of Essex is another good gunk hole and birding spot at Goose Island and Lord Cove [4.0]. Dinghies and canoes can wander all over this area, but deeper-draft boats should keep an eye on the charts and not go any farther into Lord Cove than the northeast corner of Goose Island.

Just south of Goose Island is Calves Island [3.5], which is another good, quiet place to drop anchor or spend some time with field glasses in hand enjoying the flora and fauna.

The Baldwin Bridge, Rte. I-95 [3.0], is ½ mile down from Goose Island. It has a vertical clearance of 81 feet. The state of Connecticut maintains an access ramp underneath the bridge in Old Saybrook.

Immediately upstream of the railroad bridge, the Connecticut Department of Environmental Protection has purchased land at Ferry Point on the east side of the River in Old Lyme. A state park with boat launching and picnicing facilities is planned. The Marine Fisheries Program will also have its headquarters here.

The AMTRAK railroad bridge is at mile 2.0. The bridge is usually in the "up" position since there is more river traffic than rail traffic. When the bridge is in the "down" position, there is 19 feet of vertical clearance under the central span. If this is insufficient clearance for you to pass, blow a long and a short blast of your horn. The bridge operator does not usually respond to sound signals; however, if he does, a long and a short blast means that the bridge will open shortly. A five second blast indicates that the bridge cannot open. You can also contact the bridge tender on VHF ch. 13. Smaller boats without clearance problems need not pass through the drawbridge (main channel) span; there is sufficient water depth under most of the rest of the spans. In fact, avoiding the drawbridge congestion so common on summer weekends is a good idea.

The Lieutenant River enters from the east immediately after the AMTRAK bridge. Canoes and small outboards can go 1½ miles up this tributary to the town of Old Lyme, and another 1½ miles to a lakelike area. You can also use the entrance to the Lieutenant River as an entrance to a large cove north of Great Island. These marshes and backwater support a sizable population of osprey and other fishing birds.

There are two town landings in Old Lyme that can be reached off Smith's Neck Road. There is sufficient water in the Back River and the Black Hall River for runabouts, but you must pay close attention to the tides. Old Lyme is one of the most beautiful of the River towns, with many fine old sea captains' houses. It was also a well-known artists' colony in the early 20th century. The Florence Griswold Museum in Old Lyme has an outstanding collection of American Impressionists' paintings and is a very pleasant way to spend an afternoon (203) 434-5542.

On the west side of the River are the North and South coves of Old Saybrook. The channel into the North Cove is about 100 feet wide and 4¹/₂ feet deep. A rectangular basin has been dredged out of the very shallow cove, so don't go too close to the edges. It is a well-protected spot, and there is fair holding on the bottom. Very little space is available for anchoring, and then only on short scope because of the number of boats that are permanently moored here. The town and the North Cove Yacht Club each maintains a guest mooring at the head (west end) of the cove. The town of Old Saybrook has a small dock at the western end of the cove.

Between the North and South coves is Saybrook Point, where Saybrook Fort was established in 1635 under the command of Lion Gardiner, a statue of whom is in nearby Saybrook Fort Monument Park. A stone tablet marks the site of Yale College, which was located in Saybrook from 1707 to 1716. Regularly scheduled cruises onboard *The Lady Fenwick* leave from the dock at Saybrook Point during the summer and fall.

South Cove has a submerged and ruined railroad causeway across its mouth and a new road causeway across its middle. You can have fun fishing in here from your canoe or dinghy, but don't try it from anything larger.

Finally, you come to the mouth of the 410-mile "Quinnehtqut" River at the Saybrook Lighthouse on Lynde Point. It is here that the Dutch sailor Adrian Block began his famous journey up the "long tidal river" to Enfield in his 44-foot boat, the *Onrust,* in the year 1614.

The River's mouth is comparatively shallow. In fact, the constantly shifting shoals and sandbars here hindered colonial navigation and prevented the early establishment of a deep-water port. Even today the Connecticut River is one of the few American rivers of its size without a major city at its mouth. Thanks to the sandbars, the River's estuary has remained relatively unspoiled and free of industrial development.

Needless to say, boaters should watch the tides and exercise caution when navigating the shallows on the eastern side of the River's mouth off Griswold Point. The main channel exits through two stone breakwaters on the western side beyond Saybrook Point Lighthouse.

THE CONNECTICUT RIVER STEAMBOATS

Essex's Steamboat Dock, now the Connecticut River Museum, and Goodspeed's Landing in East Haddam are two of the few remaining landings left from the days when the great steamboats ran the Connecticut River. Regular service from Hartford to New York, and places in between, began in 1822 and lasted until 1931. At first small and awkward, the steamboats grew in size, speed, and luxuriousness, becoming floating palaces bedecked with velvet and crystal. One of the last of the fleet, the *Middletown*, was 243 feet long, 145 feet wide, with 1,554 gross tonnage. It had accommodations for 350 passengers. The steamboats formed an important link for the River towns and the large metropolitan areas of New York and Boston. The smooth ride of a steamboat was also much preferred to the bouncy and slow stage coaches.

These beautiful boats also had their share of troubles. The *Ellsworth*'s boiler exploded off Essex in 1827, as did the *New England*'s in 1933. The *City of Hartford* hit both the Lyme and Middletown railroad bridges. The *State of New York* caught fire at East Haddam in 1881, followed by the *Granite State* at the same location two years later. The best of the steamboat years were from 1892 to 1917. Thereafter, competition from the railroads and the automobile sealed their doom. The last steamboat trip on the River was made by the *Hartford* on October 31, 1931 ◆

City of Hartford *collided with the Middletown*
railroad bridge, March 29, 1876.

ALBERT EINSTEIN

One of the many vacationers to visit Lyme and the lower Connecticut River during the summer of 1935 was Albert Einstein. Having sailed on a small inland lake near Berlin, he decided to rent a Cape Cod Knockabout to sail on the River. Unfamiliar with the intricate currents, sandbars, and tides, he was said to have spent more time aground than afloat. *The New London Day* wrote about his misadventures under the headline, "Einstein's Miscalculation Leaves Him Stuck on Bar of Lower Connecticut River" ◆

Lynde Point Lighthouse, Old Saybrook, CT.

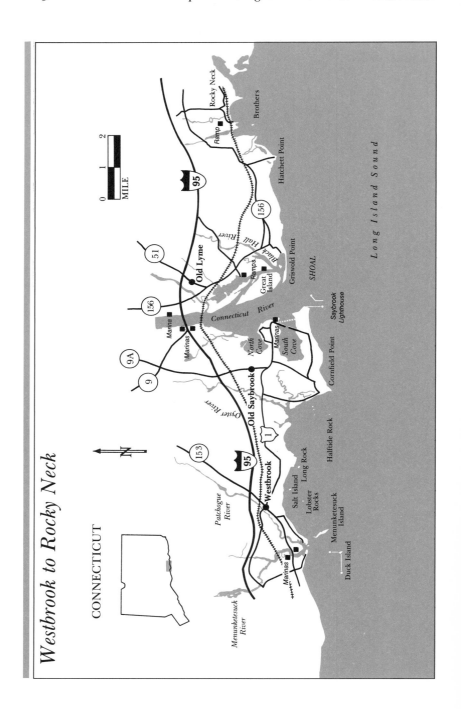

Westbrook to Rocky Neck

CONNECTICUT

N

Long Island Sound

Rocky Neck

Brothers

Ramp

95

Hatchett Point

156

51

Hall River

Old Lyme

Griswold Point

156

SHOAL

Ramps

Great Island

Connecticut River

Marina

Marinas

North Cove

Saybrook Lighthouse

9A

Marinas South Cove

9

Cornfield Point

Oyster River

Old Saybrook

Halftide Rock

1

153

Long Rock

Westbrook

95

Salt Island

Lobster Rocks

Menunketesuck Island

Patchogue River

Duck Island

Marinas

Menunketesuck River

0 1 2
MILE

Westbrook to Rocky Neck

MILE:	To Westbrook: 6.3 nautical miles.
	To Rocky Neck: 5.4 nautical miles.
NAVIGABLE BY:	Cruising boats; power and sail.
	Smaller craft in calm weather.
DIFFICULTY:	Ocean: Beware of tides, high winds, and large waves.
PORTAGES:	None.
CAMPING:	Rocky Neck State Park; Niantic, CT 06357.
	Box 676, (203) 739-5471.
USGS:	Essex 7.5,
	Old Lyme 7.5,
	Niantic 7.5.
NOAA:	Connecticut River:
	Long Island Sound to Deep River (#12375).
	North Shore of Long Island:
	Duck Island to Madison Reef (#12374).
	North Shore of Long Island Sound:
	Niantic Bay and Vicinity (#13211).
	Eastern Long Island:
	Stratford Point to New London (#12354).
RECOMMENDED:	Tidal Currents Tables; Atlantic Coast of
	North America (Dept. of Commerce) or
	Eldridge Tide Tables.

With the land mass of Long Island acting as a buffer, the Connecticut shoreline and the Sound are excellent areas for boating. The number of brilliant white sails that can be seen on the Sound on a clear day in July is testament to the popularity of the area. Prudence, however, is recommended. While windsurfers and kayaks have been seen in the Sound well off the mouth of the Connecticut River, these craft are not suitable for safe operation in open water, particularly if the wind and current are opposed.

From Saybrook Point west to Westbrook

Where it empties into the Sound, the Connecticut River is over a mile wide and, for three-fourths of its width, only a few feet deep. The navigable channel to open water lies between the two breakwaters on the Old Saybrook side. These are easily identified at a distance by the two lighthouses on the western breakwater: Lynde Point Lighthouse, the inner, taller light built in 1803, and the outer lighthouse, Saybrook Light, a modern automated structure with a fog signal. Be on the lookout for commercial traffic entering and leaving the River, and—especially on weekends—watch out for the wakes of large powerboats.

Stay well beyond the lobster-pot markers off the breakwater before turning westerly for the offshore light buoy marking Cornfield Point shoal. The point itself can be recognized by the sprawling, red-roofed Castle Inn at Cornfield Point. There is a passage inside the shoal very close to shore with a least depth of 15 feet. It is more interesting than the trip outside, but it requires careful navigation and a sharp lookout for Halftide Rock. Usually awash, the rock shows a day mark. This and other obstacles are clearly marked on the charts.

As you approach Westbrook, your landmark will be the stone jetties that head north and west of Duck Island, known as Duck Island Roads. Leaving Menunketesuck Island well to starboard, steer for the narrow, buoyed entrance to Westbrook Harbor—actually the Patchogue and Menunketesuck rivers. Pilot's Point Marina, the largest marina covered in this book, is located here, with 850 slips. You can contact the marina at (203) 399-7906 or on VHF channel 16. In Westbrook you will find enough restaurants, chandleries, grocery stores, and Laundromats, etc. to stock your belly, tool box, ice chest, or hamper. There is also a public beach nearby.

The channel into the various marinas is 8 feet deep, narrow, and can have a swift current. The Rte. 1 bridges prematurely cut off the rivers to sailboats and large powerboats, but many smaller powerboats are docked well upstream.

If, after victualing, you'd prefer to spend the night away from the clamor of too many marina neighbors, the area inside the jetties at Duck Island Roads is a good anchorage in a southwest wind. The anchorage is uneasy in a northern blow. There is OK holding on the bottom. Here, as elsewhere, there are mine fields of lobster pots to cope with, both underway and at anchor. They are a terrible nuisance. On the other hand, the lobsters in the pounds near the Rte. 1 bridges are plentiful and relatively inexpensive.

From Saybrook Point east to Rocky Neck

The water just off the Connecticut River breakwaters is very shallow. Curb any urge to leave the River and immediately turn left. If you draw less than 4 feet, stand out about 1/2 mile and slowly come east to a heading that will clear Griswold Point. If you draw over 4 feet, it would be wise to stand a mile offshore to Bell "8" before making for Griswold Point.

Hatchett Reef is the principal hazard on the passage to Rocky Neck. It is well marked and there is plenty of water between it and the mainland, so don't hesitate to take the inside route, north of the shoal. There are still undeveloped beaches along this shore and a large variety of birds. You will pass Soundview, Hatchett Point, and East Lyme.

Keep an eye on the chart as you approach Black Point—the prominent peninsula dead ahead—and locate the Brothers, a cluster of small rocky islands inshore to port. Pass either side of the Brothers to reach the jetty at Rocky Neck State Park. The park is identified by the pavilion atop the hill north of the jetty. If you are a lover of beaches, sink your toes in here.

DAVID BUSHNELL
AND *THE AMERICAN TURTLE*

It is fitting, although only a coincidence, that the nation's submarine fleet is based in the home state of the submarine's inventor: David Bushnell of Westbrook, CT. Born in 1740, Bushnell entered Yale at the age of 31. During his senior year, he astonished classmates and professors by exploding two ounces of gunpowder underwater. At the time of Bushnell's graduation in 1775, hostilities between the American colonies and the British were growing steadily. Bushnell's patriotism led him to apply his knowledge of underwater explosives to the development of underwater mines and a means of getting them to their targets. The result was *The American Turtle*, the first successful submarine.

Bushnell's submarine was named *The American Turtle* because it resembled two tortoise shells bolted together. It was built of oak and steel similar to a large wine cask, and was propelled by means of hand-driven propellers. It could submerge or rise by turning a vertical propeller or by pumping water into or out of the bilge. The operator navigated by the phosphorescent tips of a compass and depth gauge. *The American Turtle* was also outfitted with a sharp steel screw that could be screwed into the bottom of enemy ships. A mine with a timing device was attached to the screw and set to detonate after the submarine had escaped.

Bushnell made the first trial run of *The American Turtle* on the Connecticut River off Ayer's Point. He was then sent by General George Washington to New York Harbor to sink the 64-gun British flagship, *The Eagle*. Unfortunately, the usual operator of the submarine fell sick and had to be replaced by an inexperienced Ezra Lee. Lee managed to get under *The Eagle,* but was unable to attach the mine. As daybreak was coming, he decided to retreat and try again another night. However, his retreat was seen by the British and in order to escape, he set off the mine, keeping the British at bay, but revealing to them the intentions of the strange Yankee craft. *The American Turtle* went on several other missions, all with similar results.

Perhaps Bushnell did not receive the credit he deserves because *The American Turtle* did not succeed in sinking any major British ships or because of Bushnell's own secrecy. Bushnell's lack of recognition may also be because Robert Fulton later laid claim to the invention and had to be publicly denounced by Thomas Jefferson. Fulton did, however, succeed in taking credit for the invention of the steamboat, which was, in fact, developed by John Fitch of South Windsor, CT, and by Samuel Morey of Orford, NH ◆

WLIS 1420 AM

P L A N   Y O U R   D A Y

WEATHER INFORMATION
TWICE EACH HOUR

MUSIC SPORTS NEWS

WLIS 1420-AM
Old Saybrook

THE BORDER DISPUTE BETWEEN LYME & NEW LONDON

In the 1670's there was a long-standing boundary dispute between New London and Lyme over a 4-mile strip of land. In the words of Timothy Dwight:

"New London proposed to take three miles in width, and leave one to Lyme. Lyme made a similar proposal to New London. . . . In this situation, the inhabitants of both townships agreed to settle their respective titles to the land in controversy by a combat between two champions to be chosen by each for that purpose. New London selected two men by the names of Picket and Latimer. Lyme committed in its cause to two others, named Grisold and Ely. On a day mutually appointed, the champions appeared in the field, and fought with their fists, till victory declared in favor of each of the Lyme combatants. Lyme then quietly took possession of the controverted tract, and has held it undisputed to the present day."

From *Connecticut Recollections*, John Barber, 1836 ◆

Great Island, Old Lyme, CT.

Emergency Aid Locations

We have provided the following list of hospitals in case an accident happens and medical assistance is needed in a hurry. The list is arranged to follow the chapters of this book, New Hampshire and Vermont, Massachusetts, and Connecticut, and is arranged from north to south. To save valuable time in an emergency, you should look over this list before you leave for your trip so that you are familiar with the listings if the need should arise. We have also provided River mile reference numbers to assist you in determining which hospital is closest.

New Hampshire and Vermont

[311] Lancaster, NH 03584
Beatrice D. Weeks
 Memorial Hospital
Middle Street
(603) 788-4911

[288] Littleton, NH 03561
Littleton Hospital
107 Cottage Street
(603) 444-7731

[265] Woodsville, NH 03785
Cottage Hospital
Swiftwater Road
(603) 747-2761

[214] Hanover, NH 03755
Mary Hitchcock
 Memorial 'Hospital
2 Maynard Street
(603) 643-4000

[211] White River Junction, VT
 05001
Veterans Administration
 Center
North Hartland Road
(802) 295-9363

[211] Lebanon, NH 03766
Alice Peck Day Memorial
 Hospital
125 Mascoma Street
(603) 448-3121

[197] Windsor, VT 05089
Mt. Ascutney Hospital
Country Road
(802) 674-6711

[192] Claremont, NH 03743
Valley Regional Hospital
243 Elm Street
(603) 542-7771

[180] Springfield, VT 05156
Springfield Hospital
25 Ridgewood Road
(802) 885-2151

[170] Bellows Falls, VT 05101
Rockingham Memorial
 Hospital
Hospital Center
(802) 463-3903

[160] Keene, NH 03431
Cheshire Hospital
580 Court Street
(603) 352-4111

[153] Townshend, VT 05345
Grace Cottage Hospital
Route 35
(802) 365-7920

[144] Brattleboro, VT 05301
Brattleboro Memorial
 Hospital
9 Belmont Ave.
(802) 257-0341

Massachusetts

[117] Turner's Falls, MA 01376
Farren Memorial
Hospital
56 Main Street
(413) 774-3111

[115] Greenfield, MA 01301
Franklin Medical Center
164 High Street
(413) 772-0211

[92] Northampton, MA 01060
Cooley-Dickinson
Hospital
30 Locust Street
(413) 584-4090

[81] Holyoke, MA 01040
Holyoke Hospital
575 Beech Street
(413) 536-5221

[81] Holyoke, MA 01040
Providence Hospital
1233 Main Street
(413) 536-5111

[71] Springfield, MA 01107
Baystate Medical Center
679 Chestnut Street
140 High Street
(Wesson unit)
(413) 787-2500

[71] Springfield, MA 01164
Mercy Hospital
271 Carew Street
(413) 781-9100

[71] Springfield, MA 01109
Springfield Municipal
Hospital
1400 State Street
(413) 787-6700

Connecticut

[54] Bloomfield, CT 06002
Mount Sinai Hospital
500 Blue Hills Avenue
(203) 242-4431

[49] Hartford, CT 06105
St. Francis Hospital
114 Woodland Street
(203) 548-4000

[49] Hartford, CT 06115
Hartford Hospital
80 Seymour Street
(203) 524-3011

[30] Middletown, CT 06457
Middlesex Memorial
Hospital
Crescent Street
(203) 344-6720

[6] Essex, CT 06426
Shoreline Clinic
(Division of Middlesex
Memorial Hospital)
Route 153
(203) 767-0107

[   ] New London, CT 06320
Lawrence & Memorial
Hospital
Montauk Ave.
(203) 442-0711

State Agencies

Connecticut

Department of Environmental Protection
165 Capitol Avenue
Hartford, CT 06106

Boating Safety Commission
State Office Building
Hartford, CT 06106

Massachusetts

Division of Fisheries and Wildlife
Field Headquarters
Westboro, MA 01581

Division of Motor Boats
100 Nashua Street
Boston, MA

New Hampshire

Department of Fish and Game
34 Bridge Street
Concord, NH 03301

Department of Resources and
    Economic Development
P.O. Box 856
Concord, NH 03301

Department of Safety
Division of Safety Services
Concord, NH 03301

Vermont

Office of Vacation Travel
Montpelier, VT 05602

Department of Fish and Game
Agency of Environmental Conservation
Montpelier, VT 05602

Department of Public Safety
Marine Division
Montpelier, VT 05602

Bibliography

AMC River Guide: Central/Southern New England—Volume 2. Boston, MA: The Appalachian Mountain Club, 1978.

Canoeing on the Connecticut River. Montpelier, VT: Vermont State Board of Recreation and Water Resources Department, 1964.

Delaney, Edmund T., *The Connecticut River: New England's Historic Waterway.* Chester, CT: The Globe Pequot Press, 1983.

Grant, Marion Hepburn, *The Infernal Machines of Saybrook's David Bushnell.* Old Saybrook, CT: The Bicentennial Committee of Old Saybrook, Connecticut, 1976.

Jacobus, Melanethon W., *The Connecticut River Steamboat Story.* Hartford, CT: The Connecticut Historical Society, 1956.

Schweiker, Roioli, *Canoe Camping Vermont and New Hampshire Rivers.* Somersworth, NH: New Hampshire Publishing Company, 1977.

Wikoff, Jerold, *The Upper Valley: An Illustrated Tour Along the Connecticut River Before the Twentieth Century.* Chelsea, VT: Chelsea Green Publishing Company, 1985.

Illustration Credits

Cover illustrations and maps by Robert Sorensen

Page

Index

Index to Advertisers

CONNECTICUT RIVER WATERSHED COUNCIL, Inc.
125 Combs Road . Easthampton . MA 01027

I wish to join the effort to restore and conserve the natural resources of the Connecticut River Watershed through membership in the Council.

NAME _____

ADDRESS _____

_____

PHONE _____

FAMILY/INDIVIDUAL:
    Student $10 ☐
    Supporting $15-$24 ☐
    Sustaining $25-$99 ☐
    Sponsor $100 & Up ☐

GROUP CATEGORIES:
    Organization $25 & Up ☐
    Commercial $50-$200 ☐
    Corporate $200-$2,000 ☐

Make checks payable to the *Connecticut River Watershed Council, Inc.* Contributions are tax deductable to the extent provided by law.

YES!

I would like to order The Complete Boating Guide to the Connecticut River.

NAME _____

STREET _____

CITY _____

STATE _____ ZIP _____

	Number of Copies	Price	Total
		Non-member $9.95	
		Member $7.95	
MA residents Sales Tax 5% or CT residents Sales Tax 7.5%			
Postage & Handling $1.50 per book			
TOTAL ENCLOSED			